ED. JOHN MANNION

I Spy

Collins

An imprint of HarperCollins*Publishers*

Published by HarperCollins*Publishers* Limited
77–85 Fulham Palace Road
Hammersmith
London
W6 8JB

www.**Collins**Education.com
Online support for schools and colleges

First published 2002

Reprinted 10 9 8 7 6 5 4 3 2 1

ISBN: 0 00 713503 3

British Library Cataloguing in Publication Data
A Catalogue record for this publication is available from the British Library
Commissioning editor: Domenica de Rosa
Editor: Gaynor Spry, Nancy Terry, Mark Dudgeon
Cover design: Ken Vail Graphic Design, Cambridge
Typesetting: Derek Lee
Cover photograph/illustration: Stone
Production: Katie Morris

Printed by: Imago

Contents

Introduction

Success in the game of 'I spy with my little eye' requires you to look at the world from someone else's point of view. In the game you only have an initial letter as a clue, but in this anthology you are invited you see the world from someone else's point of view with all the help that good writing can provide.

Writing from a personal perspective is not necessarily autobiography: it can include diaries, letters, travel writing, magazine articles, and even political polemic, but in all cases the writer's thoughts and feelings are the centre of our attention. The desire to communicate seems fundamental to being human, and in two of the extracts here we see writers struggling against almost impossible odds simply to get their words on paper. Jean Dominique Bauby (page 23) had to blink each letter to an amanuensis (someone who takes dictation) whilst Christy Brown could only write with his left foot (page 27).

Some of the writers in this anthology, like Anne Frank (page 50) or Dorothy Wordsworth (page 122), wrote only for themselves or for their friends. In these cases we could be accused of eavesdropping on their lives, but we can be forgiven for this because of either who the writers were or because of the events they witnessed. On the other hand, writers like Primo Levi (page 54) and Robert Graves (page 60) wrote for publication because the events they witnessed were so important to themselves and to the rest of the world.

But if neither the writer nor the event is 'important', what makes writing from a personal perspective interesting? Sometimes we simply appreciate the writer's wit and style, as in Bill Bryson's account of queuing (page 152) or Clive James's recollections of encounters with deadly reptiles and spiders (page 40). Sometimes we can enjoy comparing our own experiences with those of others, as in the three accounts of school (pages 105–119). And sometimes writers can take us to the edge of mystery, as in Bruce Chatwin's encounter with a yeti (page 34) or they can help us to face up to some of the most important aspects of 'ordinary' life such as birth, illness and death. Lorna Sage (page 88) on childbirth, Ruth Picardie (page 67) on illness and Maxim Gorky (page 73) on death do not make for comfortable reading but they take us to areas of experience that are at once ordinary and extraordinary.

As readers we can travel through time and space to the island of Corfu between the wars, a quiet Oxfordshire village at the turn of the twentieth century or to a prison cell in South Africa under the apartheid regime. We can imagine what it is like to deal with unappreciative students, a mad mother or an over-religious father. Wherever we choose to go we have an opportunity to share another human being's thoughts and feelings, and to compare them with our own. We spend all of our lives inside our own heads but writing from a personal perspective gives us a chance to enter someone else's.

Illness and Disability

The extracts in this section demonstrate the importance of communication in helping to deal with quite terrible afflictions. Two of the writers were near to death when they wrote but felt it important to record their experiences for the benefit of others. A third author uses her ability to write to help her to cope with the death of a brother and the fourth found in writing a wonderful escape from the trap that his body had placed him in.

Meeting Francesca

Francesca Luard

THE following account is taken from Francesca Luard's book about family life. It was written shortly before her death from AIDS. In this section Francesca records her thoughts and feelings on the day she learned that she had AIDS.

THE specialist sent me for some blood tests and diagnosed tuberculosis, formerly known as 'consumption'. That was quite fun. Many of the great artists had had it, I was in good company. I didn't have any old disease – I had a big one. But it was all right, because in this day and age, you just take some medication and you're fine again. I was put on a heavy course of antibiotics which seemed to do the trick, and after a couple of months I returned to work. Shortly after that I lost my job. The industry was in recession and cut-backs were being made all over the place. I had only been half the person I normally am for about a year, so I was the one to lose my job. I can't blame anyone. In my employer's position, I would have done the same.

I continued the course of antibiotics for some months. The recommended length of treatment is between six and nine months, and after six, I felt well enough to want to come off them. I wasn't really suffering side-effects, but I couldn't drink, even at parties, for fear of interfering with the effect, and it was a bore to have to take them every day. Anyway, I was feeling better each day. Just before Christmas that year, I was allowed to stop taking them.

Christmas passed and I was starting to feel a little slow and tired. A couple of weeks into January, my glands were swelling up again. I was relapsing, and when I returned to the specialist he decided we should check and see if there was anything else going on that might be making me run-down. He suggested it might be a good idea to test for HIV, just in case, so that we could clear that possibility and begin to look for some other reason for the recurrence of the TB.

Sure, I said, good idea, and trotted around the corner to have my blood tested.

The specialist was a private doctor, so he sent me to a private laboratory. I knew the place already. The number of staff and the cleanliness spoke of money. I handed in my forms at the desk, and took a seat in the waiting-room. I was summoned by a man in a white coat. I followed him down the corridor to a boxroom containing a single chair, where he took a blood sample. And that was it. Home.

From everything I have heard since, I was the exception. The way anyone is tested for HIV now is very different. Before the test, you are given counselling to make sure you understand the implications, and that you are strong enough to be able to handle a positive result. You have to convince the counsellor you will not be alone when you get the result. You are then given the test and return later for your results and further counselling if necessary.

For me it wasn't like that. I had no counselling. Nobody spoke to me, except the accountant to ask me for the fee. It wasn't until I had given my blood and walked out of the building that I began to worry. I thought the possibility was there, however remote, that I could come out with a positive result, and maybe I should be facing it. I called my sister, who hopped on a bus and came to meet me for coffee.

The next day, I started to worry in earnest. I wasn't desperately anxious, just uncomfortable. I kept thinking it's always possible the test will come out positive. Finally, I decided that I would continue to worry until I knew the result. I called the specialist who said my anxiety was quite understandable, and he would let me know as soon as the results came through. At the time it crossed my mind that this was slightly strange because it obviously meant he would have to give me the result over the telephone. He said he would call me by eleven o'clock the next morning.

The following day, I was pottering around my flat. At ten-thirty the telephone rang. It was my mother. She wanted to know if I had heard anything. I said, in all honesty, that I wasn't really thinking about it and anyway he wasn't due to call me until eleven. I put the telephone down and shortly afterwards it rang again.

It was the specialist.

He said, "It doesn't look good."

Silence from my end of the line. "I want you to come down and see me at the Brompton Hospital at two o'clock. It sounds worse than it is." I thought – what are you talking about? How could anything be as bad as having AIDS? I put the telephone down.

My flatmate Joe was hopping about nervously, asking me if I was OK, a slightly desperate note in his voice. I was keen to get out so I didn't have to answer his questions. I grabbed my things and jumped into a cab. By this time, there were tears in my eyes.

I sobbed quietly in the back of the cab all the way to my parents' house. My mother wasn't at home – she had popped out to the shops. My father was sitting there, a glass of wine in front of him. "It'll be all right," he said.

"Well, it won't be if the doctor now tells me I have AIDS," I replied.

My mother returned shortly afterwards, and as she walked into the room, her face went completely grey. She aged ten years in the second that she saw me. It frightened me more than anything. Maybe I was slightly in shock. There was a calm atmosphere, not hysterical. When my mother recovered a little we decided to go out for lunch to kill the time before I was due at the hospital. I put on my dark glasses to try and hide my red swollen eyes. By a ghastly coincidence at the wine bar we were served by my last lover's ex-girlfriend. She may not have recognized me.

Before we left the house, my father repeatedly asked my mother to buy some boxer shorts for him on our way back. People later explained it as some kind of displacement activity to avoid facing the real issues. Later he said that it was to try and take our minds off the situation by asking us to do something slightly ridiculous.

Bellies full of chips and wine, my mother and I trotted off to the Brompton at the appointed time. I had bought a copy of *Hello!* magazine on the way and sat my mother on the bench outside the doctor's office with it while I went in, hoping it might provide some distraction.

In that poky little room, the doctor told me I had AIDS.

I asked him how long I had, and his reply was – well, two to four years, and, because I was young and relatively healthy, I would be at the long end of the spectrum. He gave me a new prescription for my anti-TB drugs and the telephone number of a nurse at the hospital who is used to dealing with people like me. He told me not to take any important decisions, no drastic action for three or four days, until I had calmed down. I realized he meant suicide. Funnily enough, at that point, it hadn't crossed my mind. What was going through my head repeatedly (and I was saying to him) was that it can't be great for him to deliver that kind of news. He said no, but that it was worse for me to hear it.

Towards the end of the consultation he left the office to get something, and my mother, who had been sitting on the bench outside, leapt up, wanting to know what was going on. She was looking at the doctor with hate in her eyes. I said: "Look mum, it's not his fault." The look stayed there.

We left the hospital arm in arm, and nipped into the pub for a whisky mac, to warm my insides. When we walked out of there and started heading home back up the Fulham Road, we bumped into my father. He said he wanted to make sure we went to buy his boxer shorts.

Afterwards, we nipped into the off-licence, and then into the record shop. I wanted to buy some mood music – Al Green. In the record shop we bumped into three friends of mine (male).

"Hi, Fran. How are you?"

"Fine. Meet my mum and dad."

I must have looked pretty odd hidden behind my RayBans on a cold overcast day in a dimly lit record shop, stinking of drink. Later, when the young man I had spoken to heard about me, I think he saw the humour in the absurdity of that exchange.

Back at home, I was crying in my mother's arms, and I said – if it doesn't get any harder than this, I can deal with it. The toughest part was putting my family, my brother and sisters through it. I know they love me. My sister Poppy drove over from her flat to my parents' house to join us. I suppose she must have known what had happened, but I don't think it's the kind of knowledge you can really take on board unless you are there to see it and hear it. Her face just crumpled up in tears when I told her.

In the early evening my brother Caspar came home from work. I took him into the sitting-room next door and told him. He just said, "Oh, my God," over and over again. His face was serious and composed. Everyone will have their own way of dealing with it, and this is his. I don't think I have ever seen him looking more handsome. My youngest sister Honey was in India, so she would not learn about it until she returned.

That evening we were all due to attend a large family dinner, and my mother was cooking for a Burns' Night supper. We decided it would be best to all go out because otherwise we would sit in a kind of morose huddle, looking at each other, not knowing what to say. I must have looked absolutely ghastly. I hovered in the background trying to avoid the dozens of family who were there to celebrate my great-aunt's eightieth birthday. It was a fairly jolly evening after all, and probably took everyone's mind off things for a while. My cousins were all looking tall and dashing.

That night I slept in my flat, my sister curled up on the sofa next door – my guardian angel. It was a comfort to have her there. I needed people around me. I did not want to be alone at any point during the day or night. The presence of other people around me reaffirmed the fact I was still here – alive. It's like a human mirror all around. That evening I started my diary from which this account is taken. I eventually fell asleep when it was light outside. I slept well.

Activities

Reading

1 What was Francesca's attitude to the fact that she had tuberculosis or 'consumption'?

2 Why was she tested for AIDS?

3 What would you say was wrong with the way that Francesca was given the news that she had AIDS? How is it handled nowadays?

4 Did Francesca's father really need new boxer shorts? Why did he keep going on about them?

5 Make brief notes about how the different members of Francesca's family reacted to the news that she had AIDS.

6 What was embarrassing about the meeting in the record shop?

7 What did Francesca need most of all to help her cope with the news?

Discussion

8 How do you think you would react to the news that you had AIDS or some other life-threatening illness? What would be the most important thing you would need to help you cope? Discuss your thoughts in a small group.

Language study

9 Francesca Luard seems very conscious of people's faces and what they show. With a partner, go through the second part of the passage and look at the way she describes people. What kind of comment does she generally make? Do you find it helps you to understand people's reactions?

10 Francesca Luard says that her account is taken from her diary. In what ways would this piece of writing be different if she had simply reproduced her diary? What might she have left out? What has been included that would not have been in the original diary?

Writing

11 Write a letter to the doctor who was responsible for Francesca Luard's diagnosis suggesting ways in which it could have been handled more sensitively.

Compare and contrast

12 Compare the tone of this account with that of Ruth Picardie's on page 67. How are their circumstances different? How have the two women responded to their conditions? What audience do they seem to be addressing?

My Brother

Jamaica Kincaid

JAMAICA KINCAID lived in America but returned to her home in the West Indies to visit her family. On one such visit she recorded the death of her brother from AIDS.

HIS death was imminent and we were all anticipating it, including him, but we never gave any thought to the fact that this was true for all of us, too: our death was imminent, only we were not anticipating it ... yet. Death was the thing that was going to happen to him, and yet every time I got on an airplane to go and pay him a visit, I was quite afraid that I would never come back: the plane would crash, or in some way not at all explainable, I would never come back.

There is a photograph of my brother in a book (an album) full of photographs collected by my husband. They are family photographs and they are in this book because my husband wanted to give our daughter a snapshot view of the first five years of her life. The photograph of my brother that is in this album shows a young man, beautiful and perfect in the way of young people, for young people are always perfect and beautiful until they are not, until the moment they just are not. In this photograph his skin is smooth; his skin looks as if it were a piece of precious fabric covering a soft surface (the structure that was his face), and if this fabric were to be forcefully pressed with the ball of a finger, it would eventually return to its smooth and shiny surface, looking untouched by experience of any kind, internal or external. He was beautiful then. He did unspeakable things then; at least he could not speak of them and I could not really speak of them to him. I could name to him the things he did, but he could not name to me the things he did. He stole from his mother (our mother, she was my own mother, too, but I was only in the process of placing another distance between us, I was not in the process of saying I know nothing of her, as I am doing now), he stole from his brothers; he would have stolen from me too, but the things he could steal from me were not available to him: my possessions were stored on a continent far away from where he lived. He lied. He stole, he lied, and when I say he did unspeakable things, just what do I mean, for surely I know I have lied and once I stole stationery from an office in which I worked. His unspeakable things were things he was unable to speak openly about. He could never say that anything in front of him was his own, or that anything in front of him came to him in a way that he did not find humiliating. He was a thief, he was not proud to say that most of what he had had come to him through stealing. In the place in which he lived when his skin was smooth and unblemished – he was really young then but beyond adolescence – he had some books on a shelf; they were school textbooks and one was a history of the West Indies, though really it was a history of the British West Indies. This book was a book he took from his school. I understood that, taking a book from school; when I was a little girl, living on that small island, I used to steal books from the library, not my school, but the library; the school that I attended had no books that I wanted to steal. I would not have wanted to steal a book about history; I stole only novels, and all the novels I stole were novels I had read, they were all written in the nineteenth century. I was not interested in history then, only so now; my brother had history books on his shelf. He was obsessed with the great thieves who had inhabited his part of the world, the great hero-thieves of English maritime history: Horatio Nelson,[1] John Hawkins,[2] Francis Drake.[3] He thought that the thing called history was an account of significant triumphs over significant defeats recorded by significant people who had benefited from the significant triumphs; he thought (as do I) that this history of ours was primarily an account of theft and murder ("Dem tief, dem a dam tief"), but presented in such a way as to make the account seem inevitable and even fun: he liked the costumes of it, he liked the endings, the outcomes; he liked the people who won, even though he was among the things that had been won. But his life was real, not yet a part of history; his reality was that he was dead but still alive; his reality was that he had a disease called AIDS. And no matter what anyone says, or for that matter what anyone has discovered so far, it seems to me that to be so intimately acquainted with the organism that is the HIV virus is to be acquainted with death. We are all acquainted with death;

---

[1] ***Horatio Nelson:*** 1758–1805, British naval commander. He became rear admiral in 1797 after the battle of Cape St Vincent and in 1798 almost destroyed the French fleet at the battle of the Nile. He was killed at Trafalgar (1805) after defeating a combined French and Spanish fleet.

[2] ***John Hawkins:*** 1532–95, English naval commander and slave trader and treasurer of the navy (1577–89). He was commander of a squadron in the fleet that defeated the Spanish Armada (1588).

[3] ***Francis Drake:*** 1540–96, English navigator and buccaneer, the first Englishman to sail around the world (1577–80). He commanded a fleet against the Spanish Armada (1588) and contributed greatly to its defeat.

each moment, each gesture, holds in it a set of events that can easily slide into realities that are unknown, unexpected, to the point of shock; we do not really expect these moments; they arrive and are resisted, denied, and then finally, inexorably, accepted; to have the HIV virus is to have crossed the line between life and death. On one side, there is life, and the thin shadow of death hovers over it; and on the other, there is death with a small patch of life attached to it. This latter is the life of AIDS; this was how I saw my brother as he lay in his bed dying.

Activities

Reading

1 What is the difference, according to the opening paragraph, between an AIDS sufferer and a healthy person with regard to death?

2 Jamaica Kincaid says that her brother's face looked 'untouched by experience of any kind, internal or external'. Do you think his face reflected his character or was his appearance deceptive?

3 The author's brother is a thief – how can we tell that he is not proud of what he does?

4 Why does her brother enjoy reading about men such as Hawkins, Drake and Nelson?

5 What do you think the author means when she says 'his reality was that he was dead but still alive'?

Discussion

6 If you knew you were going to die soon, how would it affect your behaviour? Share your thoughts in a small group.

7 Jamaica Kincaid points out that we are all going to die soon, either from unexpected things like plane crashes or simply from growing old. Would you say that most people behave as if they were *not* going to die soon?

Language study

8 Jamaica Kincaid gives the impression that she is writing down her thoughts as they occurred to her. Find the section on page 19 beginning 'In the place which he lived ...' through to '... my brother had history books on his shelf.' In telling the reader that her brother had history books on his shelf, the narrator adds a great deal of detail about both her brother and herself.

With a partner, go through and try to explain how one thought or idea in this section leads on the next. Draw a spider diagram of the connections between her thoughts.

Writing

9 Describe someone familiar to you in the same manner as Jamaica Kincaid. Say what the person is like but also include the thoughts that you associate with him or her.

Compare and contrast

10 Jamaica Kincaid is the only writer in this section who deals with someone else's illness. In dealing with such topics, do you think it is important to record the experiences of those who cannot write about themselves? Or do you think that only those who suffer can really understand and describe their condition?

Locked In

Jean Dominique Bauby

Jean Dominique Bauby was a successful journalist and editor when a massive stroke took away his ability to control any part of his own body. He discovered, however, that he still had control of his ability to blink. His book, *The Diving-Bell*[1] *and the Butterfly*, was dictated by Bauby blinking to indicate each separate letter.

Through the frayed curtain at my window a wan glow announces the break of day. My heels hurt, my head weighs a ton, and something like a giant invisible diving-bell holds my whole body prisoner. My room emerges slowly from the gloom. I linger over every item: photos of loved ones, my children's drawings, posters, the little tin cyclist sent by a friend the day before the Paris-Roubaix bike race, and the IV pole[2] overhanging the bed where I have been confined these past six months like a hermit crab dug into his rock.

No need to wonder very long where I am, or to recall that the life I once knew was snuffed out on Friday, 8 December, last year.

Up until then I had never even heard of the brain-stem. I've since learned that it is an essential component of our

[1] ***diving-bell:*** an early type of diving apparatus consisting of an open bottomed metal 'bell' and a supply of compressed air

[2] ***IV pole:*** the pole that holds bags of fluids that are being fed to a patient intravenously; that is into his or her veins

internal computer, the inseparable link between the brain and the spinal cord. I was brutally introduced to this vital piece of anatomy when a cerebro-vascular accident put my brain-stem out of action. In the past it was known as a 'massive stroke', and you simply died. But improved resuscitation techniques have now prolonged and refined the agony. You survive, but you survive with what is so aptly known as 'locked-in syndrome'. Paralysed from head to toe, the patient, his mind intact, is imprisoned inside his own body, but unable to speak or move. In my case, blinking my left eyelid is my only means of communication.

Of course the sufferer is the last to hear the good news. I myself had twenty days of deep coma and several weeks of grogginess and somnolence[3] before I fully appreciated the extent of the damage. I did not fully awake until the end of January. When I finally surfaced, I was in Room 119 of the Naval Hospital at Berck-sur-Mer on the French Channel coast – the same Room 119, infused now with the first light of day.

An ordinary day. At seven the chapel bells begin again to punctuate the passage of time, quarter-hour by quarter-hour. After their night's respite, my congested bronchial tubes once more begin their noisy rattle. My hands, lying curled on the yellow sheets, are hurting, although I can't tell if they are burning hot or ice cold. To fight off stiffness I instinctively stretch, my arms and legs moving only a fraction of an inch. It is often enough to bring relief to a painful limb.

---

[3] ***somnolence:*** sleepiness

My cocoon becomes less oppressive, and my mind takes flight like a butterfly. There is so much to do. You can wander off in space or in time, set out for Tierra del Fuego or for King Midas's court.

You can visit the woman you love, slide down beside her and stroke her still-sleeping face. You can build castles in Spain, steal the Golden Fleece, discover Atlantis, realize your childhood dreams and adult ambitions.

Enough rambling. My main task now is to compose the first of these bedridden travel notes so that I shall be ready when my publisher's emissary arrives to take my dictation, letter by letter. In my head I churn over every sentence ten times, delete a word, add an adjective, and learn my text by heart, paragraph by paragraph.

Seven thirty. The duty nurse interrupts the flow of my thoughts. Following a well-established ritual, she draws the curtain, checks tracheostomy[4] and drip-feed, and turns on the TV so I can watch the news. Right now a cartoon celebrates the adventures of the fastest frog in the West. And what if I asked to be changed into a frog? What then?

[4] ***tracheostomy:*** the hole in the windpipe to allow breathing

Activities

Reading

1 How does the opening paragraph set the scene for the rest of the passage? How soon do we realize that we are in a hospital?
2 Explain, in your own words, the cause of 'locked-in syndrome'.
3 How does Jean Dominique Bauby occupy his time when he is on his own?
4 What are some of the things he thinks about?
5 What is his main 'work' of the day?

Discussion

6 Jean Dominique Bauby says that he dictates his, 'bedridden travel notes' by blinking one letter at a time. This sounds simple but the letter z would require 26 blinks. Also, the person watching would have to be aware of when each letter count ended. In pairs, see if you can blink a three-letter word to your partner. Write out the alphabet and number the letters before you begin. How long does it take? How much effort and concentration is required? How long would the extract you have just read take to dictate?
7 How would you react to being 'locked-in' like Jean Dominique Bauby? Share your thoughts with a partner or in a small group.

Language study

8 'In my head I churn over every sentence ten times, delete a word, add an adjective, and learn my text by heart, paragraph by paragraph'. Writers are often encouraged to make every word count, but Jean Dominique Bauby has more reason than most to do this. With a partner, go through the text and identify at least 20 adjectives. Write brief notes on at least three that you think are particularly appropriate.
9 Jean Dominique Bauby compares the state of his body to being trapped in a diving-bell and compares his mind to a butterfly. Explain what he means by these two comparisons. Do you think they express his situation well?

Writing

10 Write a description of your own room which includes some physical description and some account of your thoughts and feelings.

Contact

Christy Brown

CHRISTY BROWN was born with cerebral palsy. For the first five years of his life he had no apparent control of his limbs and no way of communicating with the outside world.

I was now five, and still I showed no real sign of intelligence. I showed no apparent interest in things except with my toes – more especially those of my left foot. Although my natural habits were clean I could not aid myself, but in this respect my father took care of me. I used to lie on my back all the time in the kitchen or, on bright warm days, out in the garden, a little bundle of crooked muscles and twisted nerves, surrounded by a family that loved me and hoped for me and that made me part of their own warmth and humanity. I was lonely, imprisoned in a world of my own, unable to communicate with others, cut off, separated from them as though a glass wall stood between my existence and theirs, thrusting me beyond the sphere of their lives and activities. I longed to run about and play with the rest, but I was unable to break loose from my bondage.

Then, suddenly, it happened! In a moment everything was changed, my future life moulded into a definite shape, my mother's faith in me rewarded and her secret fear changed into open triumph.

It happened so quickly, so simply after all the years of

waiting and uncertainty that I can see and feel the whole scene as if it had happened last week. It was the afternoon of a cold, grey December day. The streets outside glistened with snow; the white sparkling flakes stuck and melted on the window-panes and hung on the boughs of the trees like molten silver. The wind howled dismally, whipping up little whirling columns of snow that rose and fell at every fresh gust. And over all, the dull, murky sky stretched like a dark canopy, a vast infinity of greyness.

Inside, all the family were gathered round the big kitchen fire that lit up the little room with a warm glow and made giant shadows dance on the walls and ceiling.

In a corner Mona and Paddy were sitting huddled together, a few torn school primers before them. They were writing down little sums on to an old chipped slate, using a bright piece of yellow chalk. I was close to them, propped up by a few pillows against the wall, watching.

It was the chalk that attracted me so much. It was a long, slender stick of vivid yellow. I had never seen anything like it before, and it showed up so well against the black surface of the slate that I was fascinated by it as much as if it had been a stick of gold.

Suddenly I wanted desperately to do what my sister was doing. Then – without thinking or knowing exactly what I was doing, I reached out and took the stick of chalk out of my sister's hand – *with my left foot.*

I do not know why I used my left foot to do this. It is a puzzle to many people as well as to myself, for, although I had displayed a curious interest in my toes at an early age, I had never attempted before this to use either of my feet in any way. They could have been as useless to me as were my hands. That day, however, my left foot, apparently of its own volition, reached out and very impolitely took the chalk out of my sister's hand.

I held it tightly between my toes, and, acting on an impulse, made a wild sort of scribble with it on the slate. Next moment I stopped, a bit dazed, surprised, looking down at the stick of yellow chalk stuck between my toes, not knowing what to do with it next, hardly knowing how it got there. Then I looked up and became aware that everyone had stopped talking and were staring at me silently. Nobody stirred. Mona, her black curls framing her chubby little face, stared at me with great big eyes and open mouth. Across the open hearth, his face lit by flames, sat my father, leaning forward, hands outspread on his knees, his shoulders tense. I felt the sweat break out on my forehead.

My mother came in from the pantry with a steaming pot in her hand. Her eyes looked from my face down to my foot, with the chalk gripped between my toes. She put down the pot.

Then she crossed over to me and knelt down beside me, as she had done so many times before.

"I'll show you what to do with it, Chris," she said, very slowly and in a queer, jerky way, her face flushed as if with some inner excitement.

Taking another piece of chalk from Mona, she hesitated, then very deliberately drew, on the floor in front of me, *the single letter 'A'.*

"Copy that," she said, looking steadily at me. "Copy it, Christy."

I couldn't.

I looked about me, looked around at the faces that were turned towards me, tense, excited faces that were at that moment frozen, immobile, eager, waiting for a miracle in their midst.

The stillness was profound. The room was full of flame and shadow that danced before my eyes and lulled my taut nerves into a sort of waking sleep. I could hear the sound of the water-tap dripping in the pantry, the loud ticking of the clock on the mantelshelf, and the soft hiss and crackle of the logs on the open hearth.

I tried again. I put out my foot and made a wild jerking stab with the chalk which produced a very crooked line and nothing more. Mother held the slate steady for me.

"Try again, Chris," she whispered in my ear. "Again."

I did. I stiffened my body and put my left foot out again, for the third time. I drew one side of the letter. I drew half the other side. Then the stick of chalk broke and I was left with a stump. I wanted to fling it away and give up. Then I felt my mother's hand on my shoulder. I tried once more. Out went my foot. I shook, I sweated and strained every muscle. My hands were so tightly clenched that my fingernails bit into the flesh. I set my teeth so hard that I nearly pierced my lower lip. Everything in the room swam till the faces around me were mere patches of white. But – I drew it – *the letter 'A'*. There it was on the floor before me. Shaky, with awkward, wobbly sides and a very uneven centre line. But it *was* the letter 'A'. I looked up. I saw my mother's face for a moment, tears on her cheeks. Then my father stooped down and hoisted me on to his shoulder.

I had done it! It had started – the thing that was to give my mind its chance of expressing itself. True, I couldn't speak with my lips, but now I would speak through something more lasting than spoken words – written words.

That one letter, scrawled on the floor with a broken bit of yellow chalk gripped between my toes, was my road to a new world, my key to mental freedom. It was to provide a source of relaxation to the tense, taut thing that was me which panted for expression behind a twisted mouth.

Activities

Reading

1 Until the incident in the extract, did Christy's family have any evidence that his mind wasn't as damaged as his body?
2 How did the family treat him?
3 What attracted Christy to the chalk?
4 How did Christy feel after he had made the first chalk mark?
5 Why do you think his family reacted so strongly?
6 Why was it so important that Christy should copy the letter?
7 How did this incident change Christy Brown's life?

Discussion

8 It has been argued that people with problems as severe as Christy Brown are better off in a specialist institution rather than at home. What are the advantages and disadvantages of keeping children like Christy at home? Discuss your ideas in small groups and be prepared to share them with the class.

Language study

9 Christy Brown uses a number of very short sentences in this account. Go through the passage with a partner and identify each one. How do these short sentences affect the flow of the writing? How do they help to create tension?
10 There are only three pieces of direct speech in this passage. Where do they occur? Who speaks them? How do they help to create the atmosphere of the passage?

Writing

11 Write a short story called 'The Breakthrough' which features a moment of high tension. Use sentence length and dialogue to create a strong atmosphere.

Compare and contrast

12 Christy Brown writes here about his moment of escape from the limitations of his own body, whereas Jean Dominique Bauby (page 23) describes how he has been trapped by his. Explain as fully as you can what gives each writer some sense of hope and purpose.

Encounters with Animals

If your only experience of animals is as pets, this section will reveal them to you in a new, dangerous and mysterious light.

On Yeti Tracks

Bruce Chatwin

THE earth is a very big place and some parts of it are not adequately explored. It seems that in the wilder places there are always stories of mysterious creatures that may or may not exist, such as Big Foot in America or the Loch Ness Monster in Scotland. Bruce Chatwin encountered something in the Himalayas. But what was it?

WHAT did I, or any other Westerner, really know about the Yeti?

I knew, for example, that Yetis or similar species had been knocking about European literature since the Elder Pliny[1] (*Natural History* VII, 9) described a race of 'wild men' who lived in the Mountains of Imaeus (the Eastern Himalaya), moved with astonishing speed, and had huge feet turned back-to-front. I knew that the Sherpas,[2] too, believed that Yeti had his feet turned back. I knew that several tough-minded mountaineers, such as Eric Shipton or Sir John Hunt,[3] had not only photographed Yeti footprints in the snow, but had heard the Yeti shrieking. I also knew that Hillary's 'scientific' expedition had failed to find the least trace of the creature, had sent the Pangboche 'scalp' to America for analysis, and had suggested that the

---

1 ***the Elder Pliny:*** Gaius Plinius Secundus (23–79 AD) who wrote the encyclopaedic *Natural History*

2 ***Sherpas:*** Nepali people living on the southern slopes of the Himalayas

3 ***Sir John Hunt:*** (1910–1998) the leader of the expedition that first climbed Mount Everest (1953)

'tracks' were those of the snow-leopard or Tibetan blue bear, enlarged by the melting sun.

Of course, I reflected, it was *just* conceivable that some giant orang-outang-like ape had survived in the High Himalaya: but I, for one, was sceptical. I believed, rather, that Yeti was (for want of a better term) a creature of the Collective Unconscious. Man, after all, is the inventor of his own monsters. Babies 'see' monsters long before they are shown them in picture books. Milarepa, the Himalayan sage, 'saw' a Yeti at the entrance to his cave. St Anthony[4] 'saw' his fantastical menagerie in the Desert. Hairy 'devils' did actually 'possess' the Salem[5] witches; and only a few weeks earlier I had watched, in a school near Alice Springs, some Aboriginal children drawing an ape-like ogre from their mythology – in a continent that never saw an ape until the coming of the whites.

I believed, too, that the people most likely to 'see' Yetis were either simpletons or schizophrenics;[6] religious ascetics[7] or the very poor (both liable to protein deficiency); or those at high altitude with a diminished supply of oxygen to the brain. Perhaps Yeti was a mountain hallucination. But how could I explain this to Sangye?

---

[4] ***St Anthony:*** an Egyptian hermit and mystic (251–356 AD) who was much troubled by visions during his prolonged periods of fasting in the desert

[5] ***Salem:*** a city in North East Massachusetts and the scene of the execution of 19 witches after witch hunts in 1692

[6] ***schizophrenics:*** people who hold or maintain contradictory attitudes or emotions, without being aware of the contradiction

[7] ***ascetics:*** people who practise self-denial such as fasting, often for religious reasons

We slept under a pale moon at the yak-herding settlement of Labharma where Sangye had the key to a hut. Stalactites of soot hung from its rafters. Over the hearth there was a rack for drying cheese and, on the door, a set of claw marks.

"Probably a Yeti," Sangye sniggered: the Yeti was by now our standing joke.

The Yeti was even more of a joke in the morning when we got to Macchermo ... Sangye growled; Pasang pulled a Yeti-face, and I imitated the walk of Groucho Marx. We then climbed up alongside the Ngozumpa Glacier and came out into a blinding bright landscape of snow and naked rock and green lakes half-frozen over. On a patch of open water a ruddy shelldrake was nibbling at some weed. Elizabeth was watching him through binoculars when I happened to turn round – and blinked.

"Look!" I blurted out. "Yeti tracks!"

"Oh yeah?" drawled Elizabeth, and went on watching the shelldrake.

"Look at them!"

On the north-facing slope behind us there was a line of very strange footprints. They were each about fifteen inches long, wider at the toe than the heel, and on some you saw – or thought you saw – the imprint of a giant big toe. They approached the base of an almost vertical bank, stopped, continued on the slope higher up, and finally petered out along a rocky ridge. I reckoned that the creature had jumped at least eight feet into the air and twelve along. The tracks were perhaps a day old and had melted a little: even so, I could see that they hadn't been made by any of the usual contenders – yak, blue bear, snow-leopard, langur monkey, human or human hoaxer.

No hoaxer could have jumped that high, yet the Sherpas say that Yeti habitually jumps his own height and more. The strange thing was that its foot had scuffed the snow on the way up – unless it really was a Yeti-with-the-feet-turned-back, in which case the jumper had been jumping down.

I was sure there must be some logical explanation and called Sangye over.

"Did you ever," I asked, "on any of your treks, see anything like them?"

"Never," he said, darkly. "They were not made by men."

"Then who made them?"

"Same as Yeti."

I still have no idea what these 'Yeti tracks' were. My whole life has been a search for the miraculous: yet at the first faint flavour of the uncanny, I tend to turn rational and scientific. After this excitement, the whole party was infected with Yeti-fever and kept 'seeing things' on every mountain. On Cho Oyu we thought we saw Reinhold Messner manoeuvring across an ice-fall. He was on the mountain that day, but not where we could see him, and the 'thing' we did see turned out to be a pinnacle of rock, doubling and tripling as our eyes watered in the wind.

We camped at Gokyo and in the afternoon I climbed the summit of Gokyo Ri where, gasping for oxygen at 18,000 feet, I propped myself against a stone cairn and, while the wind ripped at the prayer-flags, gazed dully at the ring of blue-and-white peaks – Cho Oyu, Everest, Lhotse, Nuptse and, far to the east, the cone of Makalu.

The sky was all but cloudless; a stream of grey vapour crept up the valley from India, and above it, in the opposite direction, a few shreds of cumulus came blowing out of Tibet. I could see the Gyubanare Glacier snaking down from the Pass of Shangri La. And it occurred to me how easy it would be, in this incandescent atmosphere, to 'see' the real Shangri La as described by the mystics – the Valley of Eternal Youth, always lying somewhere to the North, where the houses are roofed with gold and the streambeds shimmer with precious stones.

Back at the camp, Sangye had shut himself in his tent with an old shaman[8] and the two were chanting hymns to propitiate the Mountain Gods. The shaman said that sometimes people saw a monastery floating in the middle of Gokyo Lake. At sundown it started to freeze. I had a headache and could only sleep fitfully. All night I heard, or imagined, strange rumbles and half-expected a hairy hand to rip through the roof of the tent. It was good to see the dawn and Elizabeth stirring in her sleeping-bag.

"Did you sleep?" I asked.

"No," she yawned. "I heard funny noises."

"What kind of noises?"

"Thumps."

---

8 ***shaman:*** holy man

Activities

Reading

1 List four pieces of evidence mentioned in the second paragraph for the existence of Yeti.

2 What are the three possible 'explanations' of Yeti mentioned by Bruce Chatwin in the third paragraph?

3 Read the description of the Yeti's tracks carefully and draw a diagram of its footprint. Compare your drawing with that of a neighbour's.

4 What effect did the finding of the tracks have on Bruce Chatwin's party?

5 Do you think Elizabeth really heard thumping noises in the night? Give reasons for your answer.

Discussion

6 On the one hand there is a great deal of evidence that Yetis exist, but on the other hand most of it tends to come from a place where hallucinations due to high altitudes are a common hazard. What do you think? Can so many people have the same hallucination, or does one story feed the next one? What could have made the tracks seen by Bruce Chatwin? Discuss your opinions in small groups and be prepared to report them back to the class.

7 Why do you think humanity fills the remote places of the earth with creatures such as UFOs, Bigfoot, the Yeti and the Loch Ness Monster? Are they just stories for children or do adults need to believe in something 'miraculous' or beyond the ordinary? Share your views with your group.

Language study

8 Look carefully at the sentences below:

> Of course, I reflected, it was *just* conceivable that some giant orang-outang-like ape had survived in the High Himalaya: but I, for one, was sceptical. I believed, rather, that Yeti was (for want of a better term) a creature of the Collective Unconscious. Man, after all, is the inventor of his own monsters.

Discuss with a partner why these sentences are so heavily punctuated. What effect do you think Bruce Chatwin is trying to achieve here?

9 Why do you think Bruce Chatwin records the names of so many places in this passage? Most readers will not know anything about them.

Writing

10 Using information from this extract, write a magazine article aimed at young people discussing the existence of the Yeti. Illustrate your article with drawings or use the internet to find photographs and other images.

Spiders and Snakes

Clive James

CLIVE JAMES grew up in Australia, although, given the dangers he encountered as a child, this seems to have been more by good luck than by good management.

JANNALI was not quite the bush proper, but it was certainly an outer suburb. You could walk over the next hill and be back in the sort of country that the convicts used to die in when they ran away. Not that they would necessarily have died of hunger. There is plenty for you to eat. Unfortunately there is also plenty that wants to eat you.

By now I have grown used to the benevolence of the English countryside, where there are no natural hazards beyond the odd clump of poison ivy, a few varieties of inimical mushroom, and half a dozen adders all of which wear number plates and have exclusive contracts with BBC television. Walking at ease in such an Augustan[1] context, it is sometimes difficult to remember what it was like to inhabit a land crawling with danger. I have already mentioned the bull-ants. There were also snakes. Walking to school bare-footed along dirt paths lined with banksias[2] and waratahs,[3] I was always expecting to meet one of the

---

[1] ***Augustan:*** quiet and peaceful
[2] ***banksias:*** a leathery-leaved shrub
[3] ***waratahs:*** a shrub with dark green leaves and large clusters of crimson flowers (the floral emblem of New South Wales)

snakes portrayed in the gaudily detailed charts which were hung up in the railway station and the post-office. Luckily the only snakes I ever encountered were harmless civilians: the filing clerks and secretaries of the serpentine world. But Uncle Vic caught a full-sized fighting snake right outside our front gate. It was a black snake – one step worse than a brown snake. A black snake can kill an adult if it is big enough. This one was big enough. Uncle Vic pinned it to the ground in the middle but both ends of it went on trying to get at him.

The next step up from the black snake is the tiger snake. It was statistically likely that at least a few tiger snakes were in our district, probably holed up in some shack and sending their girlfriends out to buy liquor. Over and above the tiger snake, so to speak, is the taipan. Luckily ours was not taipan country. Indeed at that time the taipan was not yet famous anywhere. Up in Queensland, in the sugar cane belt, the taipan was soon to begin making headlines and getting its photograph in *Pix.* Tiger snakes and black snakes can't compete with taipans, but they are bad enough. Brown snakes are pretty bad. Allegedly harmless snakes don't look very benevolent either. I used to think about all this a lot on the way to or from school. Whether to run fast or tip-toe silently was a constant dilemma, which I tried to solve by doing both at once.

I also thought about spiders. Two of the worst Australian spiders are the funnel-web and the trap-door. One is even more lethal than the other but I can't remember which. It doesn't matter, because either can put a child in peril of its life. The funnel-web is a ping-pong ball in a fox-fur. It inhabits a miniature missile silo in the ground, from which it emerges in a savage arc, ready to sink its mandibles into anything that breathes. The trap-door spider is really a funnel-web plus cunning, since it conceals the mouth of its silo with a tiny coal-hole door. Both kinds of spider can leap an incredible distance. A wood-pile might contain hundreds of each kind. If you even suspected the presence of either species in your garden you were supposed to report immediately to the responsible authorities. After the war an English immigrant lady became famous when she was discovered gaily swatting funnel-webs with a broom as they came flying at her in squadrons. Any one of them, if it had got close enough even to spit at her, would have put her in bed for a year.

I somehow managed to avoid meeting trap-door spiders or funnel-webs. Quite often I came face to face with a harmless relative, which Aunt Dot called a tarantula and I called a triantelope. Actually it was just a common garden spider called the huntsman, whose idea of a big thrill was to suck a wasp. The huntsman wove big vertical webs which I used regularly to walk into when heading tentatively down the back path to the lavatory after dark. Getting mixed up in the web, to which I knew the triantelope must be at some point attached, was a frightening sensation which I attempted to forestall by inching forward very slowly, with one hand held out. It didn't help.

But the real horror among spiders was more likely to be encountered in the lavatory itself. This was the red-back. The red-back is mainly black, with a scarlet stripe down where its spine would be if it were a vertebrate. Looking like a neatly rigged and painted single-seater that might once have been flown by von Richthofen,[4] the red-back had enough poison in it to immobilize a horse. It had the awkward habit, in unsewered areas like ours, of lurking under the lavatory seat. If a red-back bit you on the behind you were left with the problem of where to put the tourniquet and not long to think about it. Nor could you ask anyone to suck out the poison, unless you knew them very well indeed. I saw plenty of red-backs and actually got bitten by one, luckily not on the behind. I think it was a red-back. Certainly I told my mother it was. Once again the site of the wound was my right foot, which by this time must have been looking as if it belonged to Philoctetes.[5] My mother knelt, sucked and spat. We were both frightened but she was not too frightened to act. She must have been getting tired, however, of being both father and mother.

4 ***von Richthofen:*** Baron Manfred von Richthofen (1892–1918), commander during World War I of Richthofen's Flying Circus (the 11th Chasing Squadron). He was credited with 80 air victories before he was shot down. His plane was painted red, earning him the nickname *the Red Baron*.

5 ***Philoctetes:*** a hero on the Greek side in the Trojan War. He killed Paris, a Trojan hero, with a bow and poisoned arrows given to him by Hercules.

Activities

Reading

1 List the following snakes in ascending order of danger: black snake, taipan, tiger snake, brown snake.
2 What effect did the thought of snakes have on Clive James as he walked to school?
3 Describe the difference between a funnel-web spider and a trap-door spider in your own words.
4 When did Clive James tend to worry about spiders the most?
5 What made the red-back such a problem?
6 Was he really bitten by a red-back? Give reasons for your answer.
7 What overall impression do you get of Clive James as a boy from this extract?

Discussion

8 Do you think Clive James exaggerates the dangers of his childhood? After all he was only bitten once. Or do you think that the fear of all these creatures was stronger than the actual danger of meeting them? Discuss your ideas with a partner or in a small group. Can you remember similar fears from your own childhood?

Language study

9 Clive James uses some very striking images in this passage. What comparison does he use in relation to the following creatures:
- adders
- harmless snakes
- tiger snakes
- the funnel-web spider
- the red-back spider?

Several of the images are quite unlikely. Discuss whether you find this amusing or, possibly, slightly distracting.

10 This passage is a memoir. It consists of a series of recollections from the author's childhood but they are not told as a continuous 'story'. How has Clive James organized his memories in the passage? What techniques has he used to guide the reader through them?

Writing

11 In discussion with a partner, jot down notes about your own memories of childhood. Try to include several memories in categories such as 'pets', 'holidays', 'toys' or 'aunts and uncles'. When you have notes on three or four memories in the same category, discuss how best to put them together to make an interesting account. Write the account.

Scorpion

Gerald Durrell

MOST people will go a long way to avoid scorpions but Gerald Durrell found all animal life fascinating, especially the animals he found on the island of Corfu where he lived as a child.

"HERE, you are interested in the little ones of God; look at this that I caught this morning, crouching under a rock like the devil," [Yani] said, pulling from his pocket a tiny bottle, firmly corked and filled with golden olive oil; "a fine one this, a fighter. The only fighter I know who can do damage with his backside."

The bottle, filled to the brim with oil, looked as though it were made of pale amber, and enshrined in the centre, held suspended by the thickness of the oil, was a small chocolate-brown scorpion, his tail curved like a scimitar over his back. He was quite dead, suffocated by the glutinous grave. Around his corpse was a faint wisp of discoloration, like a mist in the golden oil.

"See that?" said Yani. "That's the poison. He was full, that one."

I asked, curiously, why it was necessary to put the scorpion in oil.

Yani chuckled richly, and wiped his moustache.

"You do not know, little lord, though you spend all your time on your stomach catching these things, eh?" he said, greatly amused. "Well, I will tell you. You never know, it may be of use to you. First catch the scorpion, catch him alive, and catch him as gently as a falling feather. Then you put him, alive – mark you, alive – in a bottle of oil. Let him simmer, let him die in it, let the sweet oil soak up the poison. Then, should you ever be stung by one of his brothers (and Saint Spiridion protect you from that), you must rub the place with the oil. That will cure the sting for you so that it is of no more discomfort than the prick of a thorn."

While I digested this curious information, Aphrodite appeared from the house, her wrinkled face as red as a pomegranate seed, bearing a tin tray on which was a bottle of wine, a jug of water, and a plate with bread, olives, and figs on it. Yani and I drank the wine, watered to a delicate pale pink, and ate the food in silence. In spite of his toothless gums, Yani tore large pieces of the bread off and champed them hungrily, swallowing great lumps that made his wrinkled throat swell. When we had finished, he sat back, wiped his moustache carefully, and took up the conversation again, as if there had been no pause.

"I knew a man once, a shepherd like myself, who had been to a fiesta in a distant village. On the way back, as his stomach was warm with wine, he decided to have a sleep, so he found a spot beneath some myrtles. But while he slept a scorpion crept out from under the leaves and crawled into his ear, and when he awoke it stung him."

Yani paused at this psychological moment to spit over the wall and roll himself another cigarette.

"Yes," he sighed at last, "it was very sad ... one so young. The tiny scorpion stung him in the ear ... phut! ... like that. The poor fellow flung himself about in his agony. He ran screaming through the olives, tearing at his head ... Ah! it was dreadful. There was no one to hear his cries and help him ... no one at all. In terrible pain he started to run for the village, but he never reached it. He fell down dead, down there in the valley, not far from the road. We found him the next morning when we were going to the fields. What a sight! What a sight! With that one little bite his head had swollen up as though his brains were pregnant, and he was dead, quite dead."

Yani sighed deeply and lugubriously,[1] twirling the little bottle of oil in his fingers.

"That is why," he went on, "I never go up into the hills and sleep. And, in case I should perhaps share some wine with a friend and forget the danger, I always carry a scorpion bottle with me."

[1] ***lugubriously:*** mournfully

Activities

Reading

1 Why does Yani carry a dead scorpion around with him?

2 What impression do you get of Yani from the way he speaks?

3 What impression do you get of him from the way Gerald Durrell describes him physically?

4 Why does Yani think Gerald Durrell will be interested in his story about a scorpion?

5 How well do think Yani tells his story? Give reasons for your answer.

Discussion

6 Some people find insects and 'creepy-crawlies' fascinating. Others find them horrible. Share your opinions in a small group. Have your feelings changed since you were young? What is it about such creatures that makes them so attractive or repellent?

7 Look again at Yani's account of the shepherd. Since the point of the story is that the shepherd died alone, Yani could not have known all the details. Discuss with a partner which parts of the story he could have worked out from seeing the body and which parts he made up for the sake of a good story. Do any of the details seem at all unlikely?

Language study

8 Yani is clearly a very skilled speaker of English as well as a good storyteller. What techniques, such as comparison, similes and repetition, can you find in his tale? Choose one example of each technique and say how it helps his story to come alive.

9 Apart from his name and the setting, what *linguistic* evidence can you find that Yani is not a native English speaker? Look through his words with a partner and talk about what a native English speaker would have said.

Writing

10 Yani's story from real life consists of a mixture of facts and reasonable suppositions – that is, he has made up the parts of the story he does not know for sure using his common sense. Use this technique to tell a real life story of your own. You could, for instance, 'fill in the gaps' of a story from your childhood, or you could attempt an imaginative retelling of a recent event.

Compare and contrast

11 The writers in this section all deal with powerful, dangerous or mysterious animals. Which writer has made the animals seem most real? Explain your choice.

War

Few ordinary people get to take part in extraordinary events, but in wars almost everyone does: either as soldiers living amongst the daily horrors of fighting or as victims of man's inhumanity to man. The writers in this section report on war not in terms of battles and victories but as a day-to-day brutal reality.

Arrests

Anne Frank

ANNE FRANK'S family were Dutch Jews who went into hiding during the Nazi occupation of Holland in the Second World War. Anne kept a diary of her experiences which describes life with a small group of people living in constant fear in a confined space. The Frank family were eventually arrested and sent to a concentration camp. Anne did not survive.

Friday 9 October 1942

Dear Kitty,

Today I have nothing but dismal and depressing news to report. Our many Jewish friends and acquaintances are being taken away in droves. The Gestapo[1] is treating them very roughly and transporting them in cattle-trucks to Westerbork, the big camp in Drenthe to which they're sending all the Jews. Miep told us about someone who'd managed to escape from there. It must be terrible in Westerbork. The people get almost nothing to eat, much less to drink, and there's only one lavatory and sink for several thousand people. Men and women sleep in the same room, and women and children often have their heads shaved. Escape is almost impossible; many people look Jewish, and they're branded by their shorn heads.

If it's that bad in Holland, what must it be like in those

[1] ***Gestapo:*** German secret police

faraway and uncivilized places where the Germans are sending them? We assume that most of them are being murdered. The English radio says they're being gassed. Perhaps that's the quickest way to die.

I feel terrible. Miep's account of these horrors are so heartrending, and Miep is also very distraught. The other day, for instance, the Gestapo deposited an elderly, crippled Jewish woman on Miep's doorstep while they set off to find a car. The old woman was terrified of the glaring searchlights and the guns firing at the English planes overhead. Yet Miep didn't dare let her in. Nobody would. The Germans are generous enough when it comes to punishment.

Bep is also very subdued. Her boy friend is being sent to Germany. Every time the planes fly over, she's afraid they're going to drop their entire bomb load on Bertus's head. Jokes like "Oh, don't worry, they can't all fall on him" or "One bomb is all it takes" are hardly appropriate in this situation. Bertus is not the only one being forced to work in Germany. Trainloads of young men depart daily. Some of them try to sneak off the train when it stops at a small station, but only a few manage to escape unnoticed and find a place to hide.

But that's not the end of my lamentations. Have you ever heard of the term 'hostages'? That's the latest punishment for saboteurs. It's the most horrible thing you can imagine. Leading citizens – innocent people – are taken prisoner to await their execution. If the Gestapo can't find the saboteur, they simply grab five hostages and line them up against the wall. You read the announcements of their deaths in the paper, where they're referred to as 'fatal accidents'.

Fine specimens of humanity, those Germans, and to think I'm actually one of them! No, that's not true, Hitler took away our nationality long ago. And besides, there are no greater enemies on earth than the Germans and the Jews.

Yours, Anne

Activities

Reading

1 How do the Gestapo show a lack of respect in their treatment of the Jews?

2 What are the sources of Anne's news about the outside world? Are they all equally reliable?

3 Do you find it strange that people would make jokes about bombs dropping on their friends and acquaintances? How do people use humour in stressful situations?

4 How do the Gestapo use hostages to prevent sabotage?

5 What do you think Anne Frank means when she says Hitler took away her nationality? Is she talking about the law or does she mean something more fundamental about how she sees the world?

Discussion

6 Anne Frank says, 'I feel terrible. Miep's account of these horrors are so heartrending, and Miep is also very distraught.' If Miep's stories are so awful, why do you think Anne continues to listen to her? Is bad news fascinating for some reason? Would you like to know what was going on or would you prefer not to know the worst? Share your views with a partner or in a small group.

Language study

7 Anne Frank calls her diary 'Kitty' and writes as if she were writing to a real person. Can you find examples of her 'talking' to her diary in this extract?

8 What does Anne Frank mean when she says, 'Fine specimens of humanity, those Germans'? What is this type of expression called?

Writing

9 Write a paragraph about how you feel reading Anne Frank's diary when you know that her worst fears are in fact true and that she is going to die.

Compare and contrast

10 'The worst thing about war is that it introduces horror on a day-to-day basis.' Compare the three accounts in this section and discuss them in the light of that comment. Do they make horrific things seem normal, or do we still find them shocking even if the participants didn't?

The End

Primo Levi

IN 1943 Primo Levi formed a band of partisans to resist Italian fascism. He was captured and, because he was a Jew, he was deported to the concentration camp at Auschwitz. He survived for over 20 months before the camp was liberated.

FOR the whole day we had been too busy to remark upon the event, which we still felt marked the crucial point of our entire existence; and perhaps, unconsciously, we had sought something to do precisely to avoid spare time, because face to face with liberty we felt ourselves lost, emptied, atrophied,[1] unfit for our part.

But night came, and our sick companions fell asleep. Charles and Arthur also dropped into the sleep of innocence, because they had been in the Lager[2] for one month only, and had not yet absorbed its poison. I alone, although exhausted, could not fall asleep because of my very tiredness and illness. All my limbs ached, my blood throbbed violently in my head and I felt myself overwhelmed by fever. But it was not this alone; in the very hour in which every threat seemed to vanish, in which a hope of a return to life ceased to be crazy, I was overcome – as if a dyke had crumbled – by a new and greater pain, previously buried and relegated to the margins of my consciousness by other more immediate

1 ***atrophied:*** wasted away
2 ***Lager:*** prison camp

pains: the pain of exile, of my distant home, of loneliness, of friends lost, of youth lost and of the host of corpses all around.

In my year at Buna[3] I had seen four-fifths of my companions disappear, but I had never faced the concrete presence, the blockade, of death, its sordid breath a step away, outside the window, in the bunk next to me, in my own veins. Thus I lay in a sickly state of semi-consciousness, full of gloomy thoughts.

But very soon I realized that someone else was awake. The heavy breathing of the sleepers was drowned at intervals by a hoarse and irregular panting, interrupted by coughs and groans and stifled sighs. Thylle was weeping, with the difficult and shameless tears of an old man, as intolerable as senile nudity. Perhaps he saw me move in the dark; and the solitude, which up to that day we had both sought for different reasons, must have weighed upon him as much as upon me, because in the middle of the night he asked me "are you awake?" and, not waiting for a reply, toiled up to my bunk, and, without asking permission, sat beside me.

It was not easy to understand each other; not only because of linguistic difficulties, but also because the thoughts that weighed upon us in that long night were immense, marvellous and terrible, but above all confused. I told him that I was suffering from nostalgia; and he exclaimed, after he had stopped crying, 'ten years, ten years'; and after ten years of silence, in a low stridulous[4] voice, grotesque and solemn at the same time, he began to

---

[3] ***Buna:*** the location of the prison camp
[4] ***stridulous:*** harsh, shrill or grating

sing the *Internationale*[5], leaving me perturbed, diffident[6] and moved.

The morning brought us the first signs of liberty. Some twenty Polish men and women, clearly summoned by the Russians, arrived and with little enthusiasm began to fumble around, attempting to bring some order and cleanliness into the huts and to clear away the bodies. About midday a frightened child appeared, dragging a cow by the halter; he made us understand that it was for us, that the Russians had sent it, then he abandoned the beast and fled like a bolt. I don't know how, but within minutes the poor animal was slaughtered, gutted and quartered and its remains distributed to all the corners of the camp where survivors nestled.

During the following days, we saw more Polish girls wander around the camp, pale with disgust and pity: they cleaned the patients and tended to their sores as best they could. They also lit an enormous fire in the middle of the camp, which they fed with planks from broken-down huts, and on which they cooked soup in whatever pots came to hand. Finally, on the third day, we saw a cart enter the camp led joyfully by Yankel, a Häftling:[7] he was a young Russian Jew, perhaps the only Russian among the survivors, and as such he naturally found himself acting as interpreter and liaison officer with the Soviet HQ. Between resounding cracks of his whip, he announced that he had the task of carrying all the survivors, in small groups of thirty or

[5] ***Internationale:*** revolutionary socialist song
[6] ***diffident:*** shy
[7] ***Häftling:*** prisoner

forty a day, beginning with the most seriously ill, to the central Lager of Auschwitz, now transformed into a gigantic lazaret.[8]

In the meantime, the thaw we had been fearing for so many days had started, and as the snow slowly disappeared, the camp began to change into a squalid bog. The bodies and the filth made the misty, muggy air impossible to breath. Nor had death ceased to take its toll: the sick died in their cold bunks by the dozen, and here and there along the muddy roads, as if suddenly struck down, died the greediest of the survivors, those who had followed blindly the imperious command of our age-old hunger and had stuffed themselves with the rations of meat that the Russians, still engaged in fighting, sent irregularly to the camp: sometimes little, sometimes nothing, sometimes in crazy abundance.

But I was aware of what was going on around me in only a disconnected and hazy manner. It seemed as if the weariness and the illness, like ferocious and cowardly beasts, had waited in ambush for the moment when I dismantled my defences, in order to attack me from behind. I lay in a feverish torpor, semiconscious, tended fraternally by Charles, and tormented by thirst and acute pains in my joints. There were no doctors or drugs. I also had a sore throat, and half my face had swollen; my skin had become red and rough and hurt me like a burn; perhaps I was suffering from more than one illness at the same time. When it was my turn to climb on to Yankel's cart, I was no longer able to stand on my feet.

---

[7] ***lazaret:*** hospital for persons with infectious diseases

I was hoisted on to the cart by Charles and Arthur, together with a load of dying men, from whom I did not feel very different. It was drizzling, and the sky was low and gloomy. While the slow steps of Yankel's horses drew me towards remote liberty, for the last time there filed before my eyes the huts where I had suffered and matured, the roll-call square where the gallows and the gigantic Christmas tree still towered side by side, and the gate to slavery, on which one could still read the three, now hollow, words of derision: '*Arbeit Macht Frei*', 'Work Gives Freedom'.

Activities

Reading

1 In your own words, describe how Primo Levi felt when he realized that he had survived.
2 How long had Thylle been in prison camps?
3 How did the local inhabitants respond to the prison camp?
4 Why did prisoners continue to die?
5 How did Primo Levi feel as he left the camp for the last time?
6 What is odd about the presence of a Christmas tree and a gallows in the same place?

Discussion

7 Are you surprised at Primo Levi's reaction to surviving the prison camp? What do you think was the worst aspect of being alive when so many others had died?
8 Primo Levi, along with many other Holocaust survivors, felt a duty to record his experiences. Why do you think this was? Why is it important for today's readers to read about the Holocaust?

Language study

9 Primo Levi tends to write long complex sentences. Find the one that begins 'Nor had death ceased to take its toll' and copy it into your books, using a separate line for each sense unit. How does Levi make the end of the sentence particularly powerful?
10 Primo Levi makes occasional use of similes in this passage. Choose one and explain why you find it effective.

Writing

11 Using material from this passage, write a paragraph explaining why surviving can sometimes be worse than dying.

In the Trenches

Robert Graves

THE First World War (1914–18) began with a successful German invasion of Belgium and Northern France. However, once this advance was halted, both sides dug themselves into a trench system which stretched from Switzerland to the Atlantic along the borders of France. Attempts to break through resulted in horrific casualty figures (60 000 were killed on the first day alone of the battle of the Somme), but for the rest of the time soldiers simply had to cope with life in the trenches.

ON the way up through the ruins of Bazentin-le-Petit, we were shelled with gas-shells. The standing order with regard to gas-shells was not to bother about respirators, but push on. Hitherto, they had all been lachrymatory[1] ones; these were the first of the deadly kind, so we lost half a dozen men.

When at last 'D' Company reached the trenches, scooped beside a road and not more than three feet deep, the badly shaken Tyneside company we were relieving hurried off; without any of the usual formalities. I asked their officers where the Germans were. He said he didn't know, but pointed vaguely towards Martinpuich, a mile to our front. Then I asked him who held our left flank, and how far off they were. He didn't know. I damned his soul to Hell as he went away. Having got into touch with 'C' Company behind

[1] ***lachrymatory:*** tearful

us on the right, and the Fourth Suffolks fifty yards to the left, we began deepening the trenches and presently located the Germans – in a trench system some five hundred yards to our front, keeping fairly quiet.

The next day, at dinnertime, very heavy shelling started: shells bracketed along the trench about five yards short and five yards over, but never quite got it. Three times running, my cup of tea was spilled by the concussion[2] and filled with dirt. I happened to be in a cheerful mood, and just laughed. My parcel of kippers from home seemed far more important than any bombardment – I recalled with appreciation one of my mother's sayings: "Children, remember this when you eat your kippers; kippers are cheap, yet if they cost a hundred guineas[3] each they would still find buyers among the millionaires." A tame magpie had come into the trench; apparently belonging to the Germans driven out of the village by the Gordon Highlanders a day or two before. It looked very bedraggled. "That's one for sorrow," I said. The men swore that it made some remark in German as it joined us, and talked of wringing its neck.

Being now off duty, I fell asleep in the trench without waiting for the bombardment to stop. It would be no worse getting killed asleep than awake. There were no dug-outs, of course. I found it quite easy to sleep through bombardments; though vaguely conscious of the noise, I let it go by. Yet if anybody came to wake me for my watch, or shouted "Stand-to!", I was always alert in a second. I could fall asleep sitting down, standing, marching, lying on a stone floor, or in any

---

[2] ***concussion:*** violent shaking caused by an explosion

[3] ***guineas:*** old unit of money with a value of 21 shillings, or one pound and five pence

other position, at a moment's notice at any time of day or night. But on this occasion I had a fearful nightmare: of somebody handling me secretly, choosing the place to drive a knife into me. Finally, he gripped me in the small of the back. I woke up with a start, shouting, punched at the assassin's hand – and found I had killed a mouse which had run down my neck for fear of the shells.

That afternoon the company got an order from brigade to build two cruciform[4] strong-points at such-and-such a map reference. Moodie, the company commander, and I looked at our map and laughed. Moodie sent back a message that he would be glad to obey, but would first need an artillery bombardment and considerable reinforcements; because the points selected, half-way to Martinpuich, were occupied by the enemy. Colonel Crawshay came up and verified this. He told us to build the strong-points about three hundred yards forward and two hundred yards apart. So one platoon stayed behind in the trench, and the others went out and began digging. A cruciform strong-point consisted of two trenches, each some thirty yards long, crossing at right angles in the middle; being wired all round, it looked, in diagram, like a hot-cross bun. The defenders could bring fire to bear against attacks from any direction. We were to hold these points with a Lewis gun[5] and a platoon of men apiece.

I had the first watch that night, and periodically visited both strong-points. My way to the right-hand one took me in bright moonlight along the Bazentin-High Wood road. A dead German sergeant-major, wearing a pack and full equipment,

---

[4] ***cruciform:*** cross-shaped
[5] ***Lewis gun:*** a type of machine gun

lay supine[6] in the middle of the sunken cart-track, his arms stretched out wide. He was a short, powerful man with a full black beard. I needed a charm to get myself past this sinister figure. The simplest way, I found, was to cross myself. Evidently a brigade of the Seventh Division had captured the road, whereupon the Germans shelled it heavily. The defenders, who were Gordon Highlanders, had begun to scrape fire positions in the north bank, facing the Germans, a task apparently interrupted by a counter-attack. Wounded men had crawled to a number of these small hollows, thrust their heads and shoulders inside, and died there. They looked as if hiding from the black beard.

On my second visit to the strong-point, I found the trench already dug two or three feet down, and a party of Royal Engineers waiting with coils of barbed-wire for the entanglement. But work had stopped. The whisper went round: "Get your rifles ready. Here comes Fritz!"[7] I lay flat on my face to see better, and some seventy yards away in the moonlight, made out massed figures. I restrained the men, who were itching to fire, and sent a runner back to company headquarters asking Moodie for a Lewis gun and a flare-pistol at once. I said: "They probably don't know we're here, and we'll get more of them if we let them come closer. They may even surrender." The men seemed to be under no proper command: we wondered why. There had been a number of German surrenders recently at night, and this might be one on a big scale. Then Moodie arrived with the Lewis gun, the flare-pistol, and a few more men carrying rifle-grenades. Deciding to give the enemy a chance, he sent up a flare and

[6] ***supine:*** face upwards
[7] ***Fritz:*** soldier's slang for the Germans

fired the Lewis gun over their heads. The tall officer who came running towards us, his hands lifted in surrender, seemed surprised to find that we were not Germans. He claimed that he belonged to the Public Schools Battalion in our own brigade. When asked what the hell the game was, he explained that he commanded a patrol. So Moodie sent him back for a few more of his men, to make sure it was not a trick. The patrol consisted of fifty men, wandering about aimlessly between the lines, their rifles slung, and, it seemed, without the faintest idea where they were, or what information they were supposed to secure. This Public Schools Battalion was one of four or five similar ones formed in 1914. Their training had been continually interrupted by the large withdrawal of men needed to officer other regiments. The only men left, in fact, appeared to be those unfitted to hold commissions; or even to make good private soldiers. The other battalions remained in England as training corps: this alone was sent out, and proved a constant embarrassment to the brigade.

I picked up a souvenir that night. A German gun-team had been shelled while galloping out of Bazentin towards Martinpuich. The horses and driver lay dead on the road. At the back of the limber were the gunners' treasures, among them a large lump of chalk wrapped in a piece of cloth – carved and decorated in colours with military mottoes, the flags of the Central Powers, and the names of the various battles in which the gunner had served. I sent it to headquarters as a present to Dr Dunn. Both he and it survived the war; he is practising at Glasgow again, and the lump of chalk reposes under a glass case in his consulting room.

Activities

Reading

1 What evidence is there that the Tyneside company were 'badly shaken' by their experiences in this part of the trenches?

2 How does Robert Graves react to being shelled? What does this say about his attitude to being killed at this point?

3 Why do you think Robert Graves writes more about the death of a mouse than the death of 'half a dozen men' killed in the gas attack?

4 Draw a labelled diagram of the two cruciform strong-points Graves and his men built.

5 How did the sight of the dead German sergeant-major affect Graves? How did he overcome his feelings?

6 Why were the men in the Public Schools Battalion so badly led?

Discussion

7 Discuss Robert Graves' attitude to death and dead bodies. Do you find it shocking? How do you think his attitude developed?

8 How would you respond to some of the scenes described by Graves? Discuss this with a partner or in a small group.

Language study

9 Find the paragraph beginning 'On my second visit to the strong-point'. With a partner, discuss why you think Graves has quoted some words directly and why he has reported others. Rewrite the reported speech between Graves and the officer leading the Public Schools patrol as direct speech. Which version do you prefer? Why?

Writing

10 Choose an incident from this account and write a diary entry about it from the point of view of an ordinary soldier. Include thoughts and feelings as well as saying what happened.

Death

Writing from a personal point of view can go no further than death. In these extracts, the authors see death as a mystery, a means of escape and a source of humour. Reactions to death are, it seems, as varied as the people who face up to it.

Before I Say Goodbye

Ruth Picardie

WHEN the journalist Ruth Picardie became ill with cancer, she decided to write about her responses to the disease in a series of magazine articles. The article below is the last but one before she died.

17 August 1997

On the table next to me, collected at random from various cupboards, are half-empty tumblers of: COQ 10 antioxidant formula (one tablet to be taken twice a day); emulsified linseed capsules (three times daily); vitamin C extra (two tablets twice a day); pycegenol capsules (twice daily) and mysterious pills initialled WAAC (two tablets daily). Next to them are glass phials of bone marrow and shark cartilage (10 drops of each to be taken three times daily). There is also a packet of potassium and a handful of non-identified homoeopathic remedies (one of each daily). This, I am ashamed to admit, is just a small part of the complementary medicine[1] panic I have been in for the past ten months.

I started in October by visiting a so-called complementary guru whom I'm sure won't mind being called Dr Charlatan (his swish London clinic closed down overnight; he has now disappeared). First he got me on the

[1] ***complementary medicine:*** methods of treating illnesses which focus on the patient's well being rather than by simply treating the symptoms of a disease

aforementioned supplements, a fraction of which lurk guilty and unfinished on the table, plus a £275 drink called Yeastone which filled up half the fridge. Then he got my blood analysed by a German professor who advised me that refined sugar was poison and urged me to go on a complicated diet (vinegar bad, trout good, three-day-old eggs best of all). Finally, he got me hooked up with a computer expert-cum-homoeopath[2] for a course of 'Bicom' therapy, which meant being wired up to a laptop which positively recharged my cells. I think.

All this may sound ridiculous; but when the hospital baldies have told you, aridly, that such and such a treatment only has a '50:50 survival benefit', you desperately want to lengthen the odds. Still, complementary medicine is no picnic (principally because crisps aren't allowed). I dread to think how much I spent on Dr Charlatan and friends: his initial quote was £2 500. And even though I turned down his offer of low-level oxygen administration (machine rental £150 per week, consultancy fee £75), plus a five-week course of intravenous injections[3] twice a week, the treatment turned into a huge pressure. By February, I was in such a flap about what pills I should be taking, why I couldn't eat muesli made from raw cereals, and whether or not the Yeastone could be kept in the garden because there was no longer room in the fridge, that I decided to give up the whole thing.

This was, probably, a sensible decision. After all, I'd

---

[2] ***homoeopath:*** someone who practices homeopathy – a method of treating disease by the use of small amounts of a drug that, in healthy people, produce symptoms similar to those of the disease being treated

[3] ***intravenous injections:*** injections into the vein

always been cynical about complementary medicine and the alternative lifestyle, the sort who'd snuck into a tantric yoga class as a sneaky, low-level journalistic trick. I was the woman who had utterly failed her NCT labour (hospital induction, empty birthing pool, four foetal monitors, 20-hour labour, failure to progress beyond 8 cm, pethidine,[4] epidural,[5] emergency Caesarean, hospital-induced nervous breakdown). I'm also the person whose athlete's foot has become immune to tea tree oil. What good was alternative healthcare to me?

And yet the panic and desperate hope of a girl with cancer knows no bounds. Friends and family were desperate to help, too: which is why my shelves are groaning with New-Age books: *Sharks Don't Get Cancer; Living, Loving and Healing* (written by wise gnome with magic hands); *Full Catastrophe Living* (inspirational picture of high mountain); *Spontaneous Healing* (written by man with beard).

So what did I do? Keep up with the mainstream poison, admit that linseed and books by men with facial hair are not for me? No, silly. I embarked on a weekly Chinese herb and acupuncture regime (£50 a week), which involved wolfing 24 horse tablets a day and drinking as much horrid tea as I could stomach. I persevered for six months, because I once saw Princess Diana leaving the clinic looking thin and chic, so I reckoned I was in good hands.

As if this wasn't enough, I then started going to a healer, first at a group session in London with the vibe of a

[4] ***pethidine:*** a painkiller often used during childbirth
[5] ***epidural:*** painkillers that are delivered directly into the spinal column

crematorium (fake flowers on the walls, intergalactic organ in the background). Then I got offered a series of one-on-one appointments at the healer's rural retreat: only £50 plus VAT, crashing New-Age music and a two-hour drive each way. Fun!

Luckily, I have now come to my senses. The expense, the exhausting round of treatment, the sense of failure (I kept forgetting to bring mineral water to be healed; I would 'lose' my Chinese herbs) was part of it. But the thing that finally made me give up on beards was the revelation that complementary medicine does not work! Three months with Dr Charlatan, and the disease had spread to my bones. Six months on Golden Seal Comb and Five Leaf Amachazuru tea, and tumours developed in the liver and lungs. Three months of New-Age bonging, and I ended up with a brain tumour, despite confident declarations from all and sundry that I was on the mend. To be fair to the beards, mainstream treatment from arid white-coats has utterly failed, too, but at least it's a) free, and b) you don't have to listen to Vangelis in hospital.

Luckily, there is a third therapeutic strategy which I am developing almost single-handedly, though sadly not in a controlled trial situation at present, so fellow patients will have to find their own precious path. Essentially, after months of careful research, I have discovered a treatment that is a) cheaper than complementary therapy, b) a hell of a lot more fun than chemotherapy, and c) most important, incredibly effective! Retail therapy! By this, I mean personal indulgence or escapism of any kind. For example, my first breakthrough came when I went to see Daniel Day Lewis and Winona Ryder getting hot and horny in *The Crucible*;

during the course of chemotherapy which began the next day, I was sick only once, compared with constant vomiting first time round. Pretty conclusive cause–effect, no? Soon after, I spent the morning having a divine Jurlique facial and the afternoon at the Ghost warehouse sale: the following day, my blood count was completely normal.

Then came my major shopping breakthrough: a long consultation at the Dickins & Jones personal beauty studio with skincare god John Gustafson. Perhaps the most important retail oncologist[6] in the country, he has evolved a stellar personal skin regime based on these rare products: Sisley, La Prairie, Shiseido, Elizabeth Arden, Bobbi Brown and Prescriptives. For just £250, I started looking like a film star (compared with £250 for vile Yeastone, which ended up down the sink), despite being two-thirds through the chemotherapy course from hell.

Thanks to this highly evolved, only moderately expensive and largely side-effect-free treatment (warning: my credit card bounced earlier today), I am currently in almost no pain! My symptoms are a slightly swollen brain, but I'm hoping that today's lunch (smoked salmon bagels, crisps, extra French dressing) will have a positive effect. The other problem – my enlarged liver – I believe has been solved by my later splurge at Whistles sale (blue skirt, lilac shirt). Even if the dread organ doesn't shrink, the clever bias cutting hides most of the lumps.

So have hope, fellow cripples. My non-beard book, *Shop Yourself Out of Cancer*, is coming soon.

---

[6] ***oncologist:*** specialist in cancers and tumours

Activities

Reading

1 Make a table of the medicines Ruth Picardie was supposed to take and their daily dosages. How many pills per day would she have been taking if she had followed all the advice she had been given?

2 What three therapies did Dr Charlatan involve the author in? Which of his therapies did she reject?

3 What did Ruth Picardie's second round of alternative therapies involve?

4 Did any of the alternative therapies do her any good? Did conventional medicine do her any good? Which kind of treatment did she prefer? Why?

5 What 'proof' does Ruth Picardie offer that retail therapy works?

6 In what way would you say that retail therapy really works?

Discussion

7 With a partner, discuss the tone of the article. Does Ruth Picardie take herself and her disease seriously? How can you tell? Be ready to report your findings to the rest of the class.

8 What is your reaction to Ruth Picardie's article? Do you admire her courage in maintaining a sense of humour or do you think she should not try to make illness and approaching death entertaining? Discuss your response in small groups.

Language study

9 Ruth Picardie makes use of a technique called 'metonymy' in this article. This involves using part of something to refer to it as a whole. For instance you could refer to the monarchy as 'the crown'. Identify what she means by the following metonyms:

- hospital baldies
- beards
- arid white-coats

What does her choice of metonym show about how she feels about these people?

10 Towards the end of the article, Ruth Picardie misapplies medical terms to shopping. Identify as many examples of this as you can. What is the effect of this technique? Do you think she might be poking fun at some of the books she has been reading?

Writing

11 When something unpleasant is happening people often say they will look back on it and laugh. Write a brief account of a difficult time in your own life about which you can now laugh.

Death in the Family

Maxim Gorky

MAXIM GORKY lived in Russia in the nineteenth century. At this time there were almost no effective medicines for adults, and childbirth was extremely dangerous for both mothers and babies. Some of Gorky's earliest childhood memories were of the death of his father and of his baby brother.

ANOTHER vivid experience that stands out in my memory is a rainy day in a deserted corner of a cemetery. I stood on a slippery heap of sticky mud and looked down into the pit where my father's coffin had been lowered. At the bottom was a lot of water, and a few frogs. Two of them had succeeded in climbing on to the yellow coffin lid. My grandmother, myself, a policeman who looked soaked to the skin, and two men with spades who were evidently in a very bad mood, had gathered round the grave. A warm rain, as fine as delicate beads, began to fall gently on us.

"Fill it in," said the policeman as he walked away.

Grandmother burst into tears and hid her face in her shawl. The gravediggers, bent double, began piling the earth into the grave at great speed. Water squelched. The frogs jumped off the coffin and tried to escape up the sides, but were thrown back by clods of earth.

"Let's go now, Lenya," said Grandmother as she put her hand on my shoulder. Reluctant to leave, I slipped out of her grasp.

"God help us," she grumbled – not at me, or even at God, and she stood by the grave for a long time, quite silent. Even when the grave had been levelled off she still stood there.

The gravediggers smacked their spades against the mud, which made them ring out with a hollow sound. A sudden gust of wind drove away the rain.

Grandmother took my hand and led me to a distant church surrounded by a great number of dark crosses.

"Why don't you cry?" she asked when we left the cemetery. "You *ought* to cry."

"I don't want to," I replied.

"Well, you'd better not if you don't want to," she said softly.

I found this very strange. When I did cry, which wasn't often, it was usually because of some insult, and not from physical pain; my father always laughed at me, but Mother would shout:

"Don't you dare cry!"

Afterwards we rode in a droshky[1] along a broad and very muddy street lined with houses painted deep red. I asked Grandmother:

"Will the frogs get out?"

"No, they don't stand a chance, God help them!"

Neither my mother nor my father ever mentioned the name of God so often and with such familiarity.

A few days later we were all travelling in a small cabin on board a steamboat. My newly-born brother Maxim had died and lay on a table in the corner, wrapped up in a white sheet tied round with red ribbon.

---

[1] ***droshky:*** an open four-wheeled horse-drawn passenger carriage (formerly used in Russia)

I clambered up on to the piles of luggage and trunks, and looked out of the porthole, which was round and bulging like a horse's eye. Beyond the wet glass the swirling foamy water stretched away endlessly. At times it seemed to rear up and lick the glass, making me jump back on to the floor.

"Don't be frightened," said Grandmother as she gently lifted me in her soft arms and put me back on the pile of luggage.

A grey, damp mist hung over the water. Somewhere, in the distance, a dark mass of land would loom up, and then disappear. Everything around me was shaking. Only my mother, who was leaning against a wall, her hands behind her head, stood firm and steady.

Her face, clouded over, grimly set and with the eyes shut tight, was that of a blind person. Not once did she speak. She seemed to have changed into somebody else, strange and new. Even her dress was different.

Grandmother asked her over and over again, in the soft voice she had:

"Varya dear, try and eat something, won't you?"

My mother didn't reply and remained motionless.

Grandmother used to whisper to me; with my mother she raised her voice, but all the same approached her timidly and cautiously, saying very little. It struck me that she was afraid of her. This I could well understand, and I felt all the closer to my grandmother.

"Saratov!" my mother exclaimed in an unexpectedly loud and angry voice. "Where's that sailor got to?"

The words 'Saratov' and 'sailor' were very strange and foreign-sounding.

A broad-shouldered, grey-haired man, dressed in blue,

came into the cabin. He carried a small box. Grandmother took it from him and began to lay out my brother. When she had finished she took the box in her outstretched arms to the door. But she was far too fat to get through the narrow doorway – except sideways – and her confusion and embarrassment made me laugh.

"Oh Mother!" my mother cried, and took away the coffin. They both disappeared, leaving me staring at the man in blue.

"What, has your brother gone?" he said, leaning towards me.

"Who are you?"

"A sailor."

"And who is Saratov?"

"Saratov's a town. Look out of the window ... there!"

Through the window I could see the land slipping by. It was dark and steep, and the mist rose from it in smoky rings, reminding me of a large slice of bread freshly cut from the loaf.

"And where's Grandmother gone?"

"To bury her grandson."

"Will they put him in the ground?"

"Of course. How else can they bury him?"

I told the sailor about the frogs buried alive with my father. He lifted me in his arms, gave me a firm hug and kissed me.

"You're too young to understand!" he said. "You don't have to be sorry for the frogs, to hell with them! It's your mother you should pity ... See what life's done to *her*!"

Activities

Reading

1 Which part of his father's funeral stuck in Maxim Gorky's mind the most? Why do you think this was?
2 What struck him most about the death of his brother? Why do you think Gorky reacted in this way?
3 In your own words, describe Gorky's relationship with his grandmother.
4 How does the weather contribute to the mood of this extract?
5 Why do you think the sailor was the only one to point out who was really suffering to the young boy?

Discussion

6 Discuss with a partner how old you think Maxim Gorky was when these events occurred. What clues do his behaviour and the way he was treated give you? Report your conclusions to the class.
7 The events recounted here are amongst Gorky's earliest. Share some of your earliest memories in your group. Are early memories always unhappy or traumatic ones?

Language study

8 Most of this text is in short sections. Why is this appropriate for the memories of a very young child?
9 It is unlikely that such a small child would remember everything that was spoken at these two events. Why do you think Gorky has included dialogue in his account?

Writing

10 Write down one of your own earliest memories. You should try to be as accurate as possible, but where there is a blank in your recollections try to fill it in with what is likely to have happened. Try to write as vividly as possible.

Compare and contrast

11 In what way is this account different from that of Ruth Picardie's (page 67) and Ruth First's (page 78)? Which account do you find the most moving? Give reasons for your choice.

In Prison

Ruth First

Ruth First was a white South African activist against Apartheid. At the time she was arrested the law allowed suspects to be held for 90 days without trial. In Ruth First's case she was released at the end of 90 days and then re-arrested. Here she describes the lowest moment of her imprisonment which took place shortly after she was re-arrested.

My conceit and self-centredness had at last undone me. I had thought to pit myself against the Security Branch in their own lair. What had I hoped to learn? To see dossiers carelessly littering desks, to hear the name-dropping of informants, to be taunted into giving information by the revelation, to surprise me, of what information they already had? I had been stupid. Weak. A failure. By day and by night I went over this self-exposure. I was a spider caught in my own web, spinning finer and finer threads in my head to make disentanglement impossible. I felt unimaginably tired and dispirited. I could not cope any longer. I could not weigh up factors properly. No one could get near me to help me and the help I needed could not be supplied by anyone else. I spent all Sunday making a dilatory attempt at a crossword puzzle, but filling in the clues was surface activity: a decision was forming in my mind. The Security Branch was beyond doubt planning an act of character assassination against me: I would not give them information out of loyalty to my friends, but they would break me finally with some carefully introduced indication that my friends had abandoned me because I had betrayed them, or so the Security Branch would arrange for the version to be told. This abandonment I would not be able to face; and even until it happened I did not have the strength to survive. There was only one way out, before I drove myself mad, and as the truest indication to anyone who was interested that I had not let the Security Branch have it all their own way. I was anguished when I thought of the children, but what good would I be to them in mental pieces? On the flyleaf of the crossword puzzle book, with the pencil that was the property of the South African Government, I wrote a note that apologized for my cowardice, loved the children once more, tried to say words that would have a special meaning for Joe, and indicated that I had not given in, that those still free should not panic and should proceed in the knowledge that I had kept their secrets. After the last inspection of the night I reached for the phial of pills (which the wardress had left in the cell quite inadvertently the day two doctors had called, my own and the prison one), and swallowed the lot.

I had never thought about dying so I do not know how I expected to feel coming back into consciousness. I had no feeling at being witness to my own resurrection, only a bewildering confusion of time, and place and circumstance. I thought I had moved away, but I was in the same cell. I seemed to find an easy, matter-of-fact acceptance that I had not succeeded. My mind was closed to the enormity of what I had tried to do. It might have been the same day, it might have been the one after, but suddenly the Commandant was in the cell with the wardress beside him.

"Do you want a doctor?" he asked. I nodded.

"What for? I mean what's wrong with you? Headache? Stomach ache? I have to enter something in the book."

It was Competent's[1] duty. "It's her nerves," she said shortly.

Not long after, I was afflicted by a wave of uncontrollable hysterical weeping. A prison doctor came, but I would tell him nothing and he left without discovering what anything was all about.

My weeping might have echoed through the station, or else he was snooping as usual, but then it was Viktor standing at my bedside. He took his handkerchief from his pocket and left it with me.

Days after, I assailed him for having come into the cell when I was in bed. He said, "I had to find out what was wrong." Some days after that he asked, "Were you wearing a nightie or were those shortie pyjamas?"

In the daze of coming out of what seemed like a coma I remembered to rip the message from the front of the crossword puzzle book and flush it down the lavatory.

Somehow the act of taking the pills shocked away any further intention of doing so. I had completely lost track of time and even interest in keeping a wall calendar or sewing stitches behind my dressing-gown lapel; but inch by inch I made a slow adjustment to balance, though I was not sure at the time that I was doing so. I managed to have another

[1] ***Competent:*** one of Ruth First's warders, and the name First gave her

visit from my own doctor and I told him I had taken all the pills. He was the only person I told all the while I was in prison, and I told hardly anyone when I got out. He did not seem surprised, or impressed by my surprise that the pills had not worked. "You don't think I'd be so foolish as to leave you with that size dose?" he asked, and I could laugh about my ignorance. "I'm heading for a crack-up, aren't I?" I asked, and he said, "You've had one already."

Activities

Reading

1 How, according to Ruth First's account, did the Security Branch plan to break her spirit?
2 What thought could she not stand above all else? How did she hope to disprove this?
3 How did Ruth First feel when she came round after taking the pills?
4 What did the guards think was wrong with her?
5 Why do you think Ruth First destroyed her suicide note?
6 What was the doctor's reaction on being told about the attempted suicide? How did it help Ruth First?

Discussion

7 What would be the worst part of being in prison for your political beliefs: fear of torture or physical abuse? Fear of betraying your friends? Isolation from your family and friends? Discuss these and any other ideas you may have in a small group.
8 The ancient Romans and Japanese warriors thought that suicide was an honourable form of death but it is condemned by Christianity. What is your view? Is suicide ever justifiable?

Language study

9 Why do you think Ruth First has used the single word 'weak' as a sentence in the first paragraph?
10 What effect does referring to the guard as 'Competent', rather than by using her true name, have on our view of her?

Writing

11 Imagine you have been imprisoned for your beliefs. Write three or four excerpts from your diary. The first excepts should be from early on in your imprisonment, the later ones should be after a considerable amount of time has passed.

Birth, Childhood and Parents

The Russian novelist Leo Tolstoy remarked that all happy families are the same, but that unhappy families are unique. The parents and children in the following extracts could not be described as happy but their experiences have enough in common with our own to make them interesting to read about.

Forty Weeks

Rachel Cusk

THE final stages of a pregnancy can often seem slow as the mother waits for her baby, but if things go wrong, events can move very quickly indeed.

THEN, suddenly, things change. It is February and the days are brief and pale, the nights deep and dark as lakes. The year is creaking on its hinges: soon it will open and let in the light of spring. I have been waiting for this light as for the signal of my readiness, but it never comes. A month of pregnancy remains, and I begin to bleed.

I report it to the midwife and against my protests she takes me to the hospital. Once there I am taken to the ultrasound room. A crowd gathers around my prone body. The snowy images appear once more on the screen. The sonographer leans forward, clicks at her keyboard, scrutinizes. It's unbelievable, she announces baldly. The consultant also leans forward. They probe the screen with disbelieving fingers. It's all the wrong way round, says the sonographer. The placenta is completely blocking the cervix. The baby can't come out. See? She addresses this to me. Attentively, obediently, I look, and see something black and swirling that resembles outer space. A murmur of outrage goes up. This should have been spotted earlier. It is a life-threatening condition. Had I gone ahead with my plans to have the baby at home, I am told, we would both have died. I look at the screen while they discuss it. The scanner has wandered slightly in the sonographer's distracted hand, and suddenly, out of the darkness, the sleeping face of my daughter emerges. It fills the screen, pale and tranquil as a moon, ethereal as a ghost. It is the face of a person, not putative but real, hovering, coming in, waiting to exist. No one else notices it. The sonographer gestures in the air with the scanner and it is gone.

I am told I must now remain in hospital. Rebelliously, desperately, I discharge myself and go home. The next day I come back and surrender. It is a Sunday evening. The hospital is dark and deserted, as if its customers observed office hours. A militant junior doctor keen to practise inserting things into veins falls upon me hungrily. She offers blood tests, the implantation of a canula.[1] I refuse them. Quietly enraged, she disappears and returns with back-up. It is explained to me that I must undergo these procedures. I argue and eventually submit to the blood tests alone. The junior doctor stabs the needle into my arm as if she were playing championship darts. Then she stabs it into the other arm. Blood seeps under the skin to form two large red patches, like birthmarks, up my arms. Chastened, I am put to bed in a ward. I spend the next three days there, and am visited by gangs of junior doctors who have heard about the canula incident and want to exact revenge. I fight them off. Eventually a tall, kind girl comes to my bed late one night. Let's just put it in, shall we? she says. I concede my hand, and she pushes the valve into a vein on the back of it and goes away. The consultant comes to see me. He has a jolly, Tyrolean look about him. If you'd been born a

[1] ***cannula:*** a narrow tube used inserted in to the skin to deliver medicine or other fluids

hundred and fifty years ago, he says, you'd be dead by now. I reply that most people would and he laughs uncomprehendingly. I am to have a Caesarean section. Which day would you like it? he asks with a smile. I opt for Wednesday. I ask whether the baby is ready to be removed and am assured that it is. He has delivered babies like kittens, like feathers, like thoughts, babies that hardly exist. I sense he would like them not to be in there in the first place, but to grow them himself in a seed tray. Mine has had eight months, apparently a decadent quantity of time for this hospital.

Activities

Reading

1 What is the problem with the placenta that means that the writer has to have a Caesarean section?
2 What is the reaction of the medical staff to the problem?
3 What does Rachel Cusk see whilst the medical staff are discussing her baby? How does it make her feel?
4 How does Rachel Cusk feel about going into hospital?
5 Why do you think she does not cooperate with the medical staff?
6 What seems to be the attitude of the consultant to delivering babies?

Discussion

7 Do you think that some medical professionals seem to treat pregnancy as a sort of illness? Should mothers be encouraged to have their babies at home or in hospital? What are the advantages and disadvantages of this?
8 Have you ever spent any time in hospital? How important were routines for the staff? Share your experiences with your group.

Language study

9 Look closely at the words that the Rachel Cusk uses to describe her encounters with the medical professionals. What attitude does she seem to have taken towards them?
10 Find Rachel Cusk's description of her baby. What techniques does she use to give a sense of its impact on her?
11 This passage is written in the present tense. What effect does this have on how you respond as a reader? Would the passage have worked as well in the past tense? Give reasons for your answer.

Writing

12 Write a report on Rachel Cusk as the patient from the point of view of one of the nurses looking after her.

Childbirth

Lorna Sage

HAVING an 'unwanted' pregnancy can often make the mother feel unwanted too, as Lorna Sage found out when she became pregnant at the age of 17.

THE time crept by all the same, the baby stretched and lunged but didn't turn over, and Crosshouses loomed. One day Grandma, visited and reanimated by her old anger, made a speech in which she denounced Vic, my father, Grandpa and all males everywhere including Clive, who'd grow up to be a hairy ape like the rest, throwbacks to a man (except for her Billy). Then she cried over me, remembering the horrors of childbirth. I refused to think about what would happen in any detail. Words like 'delivery' and 'confinement' (threats, promises) hung around in my imagination, but stayed just words. In truth I was more fearful of the hospital than of the event itself and I had evolved a secret plan (secret even from Vic) to have the baby at home – simply not to tell anyone that I was in labour until the last minute, when they'd have to call 999 and improvize kettles and clean sheets, which seemed, judging from the movies, the only props you needed. Peasants – real peasants – gave birth between one shift in the vineyards or the paddy fields and the next, didn't they?

The date they'd worked out at the clinic was 29 May and punctually at dusk on the twenty-eighth, when I was pacing restlessly in the garden tugging at weeds, the first twinge came and soon there was no question. Contractions. True to my resolve, I said nothing all evening, we went to bed as usual and although I couldn't sleep, that wasn't odd – my sleeplessness had returned with the discomforts of pregnancy, and Vic and I would read to each other into the small hours. That night it was his turn. The book we were in the middle of was John Wain's novel *Hurry On Down*, which would be fixed for ever in our memories by the grotesque coincidence of its title and the event.

It was a variant on the angry-young-man theme – a young man evading his middle-class destiny, a portrait of the artist as gag writer, recounting the string of comic misadventures that led him to this low-life calling. The jokes were laboured (ho, ho), but I laughed, let out a groan at the same time and gave the game away. Perhaps I'd lost my nerve. In any case, matters were taken out of my hands, the ambulance was called and Vic came with me for the long, bumpy and increasingly painful ride along back roads to Crosshouses. When we got there, around 3.30, I stepped down into a puddle of my own making, in a state of panic. The Sister on duty, who seemed instantly to know that I was late on purpose, briskly slapped me in the face two or three times, sent Vic off back to Whitchurch with the ambulance and hauled me into the Delivery Room.

There, time caught up with me. While the slap-happy Sister woke the doctor, I lay where she'd put me and watched the clock on the wall between my knees. Things were happening too fast. "Don't push!" she yelled (she wanted the doctor to be there) but I couldn't stop pushing, and although it felt as if I was being torn apart (I was) and the second hand loitered round the dial as slowly as it does for someone on speed, the adrenalin of my fright and my 17-year-old's abdominal muscles soon brought an end. The ruffled, sleepy Indian locum who arrived, pinning up her thick plait of hair, was too late, the Sister was already crooking my nerveless arm around a baby girl (girl!) wrapped in a blanket, her face streaked with blood (I remember thinking, whose? mine?) and whisking her away again. Then it was all over except for the stitches, which hurt like hell, so they gave me some gas and air, and left me alone until the real morning came. I watched the clock, fascinated. It was still only 4.15, the liminal[1] pre-dawn hour, and I'd never felt so awake, as though I'd died and been born again knowing how to tell the time. Ages later an orderly pushed a mop into the room and, seeing me there, brought me a cup of hot, sweet tea under telepathic orders from my mother, and I was immediately, violently sick (never mind, she said, mopping it up) and fell asleep.

I came to consciousness on the Maternity Ward, where the Crosshouses day was beginning. The regime was rigid: it wasn't only that temperatures, blood pressure, bedpans and medication were done on the dot, there were endless other rules. Hair-washing was strictly forbidden, even if you were well enough to walk to the bathroom; bathing was rationed; and make-up was frowned upon. Anything that might make you feel less wrecked and dirty was disallowed on principle, because Baby came first and by Crosshouses logic washing your hair was vanity, therefore traitorous to Maternity, morally unhygienic and dangerous. As a result, everyone had stiff, sweaty hair sticking out in tufts, some of

[1] ***liminal:*** at the threshold of a sensation, almost too faint to be experienced

it grey, for one of the offences several of these mothers had committed against order and decency was to go on having babies into their forties. By contrast the nurses, Sisters and Matron were as good as vestals, unmarried or at least childless, their baby worship was pure. They served the cause of motherhood selflessly, unlike the feckless women in their charge, who'd probably been thinking of sex, or failed to plan, and who didn't deserve babies.

So mothers were dirt and fathers hardly came into it at all, for visiting hours were brief and the hospital was nearly impossible to reach by bus. There were no public phones. The ward was the world. The babies were segregated in a nursery a couple of corridors away, where mothers weren't allowed, and where they were bottle-fed in the night and cried continuously, waking each other up. In the daytime they were handed out at four-hour intervals for breast-feeding, which had suddenly become the rule and created many more minor offences to do with having too much milk or not enough, or the wrong sort of nipples. When Matron made her rounds, I said I didn't want to breast-feed, but luckily she wasn't listening, she'd spotted down the ward an enormity, a woman with red nails. Marching smartly to the bedside she picked up the woman's hand and flung it back at her with disgust: "We don't feed our babies on nail varnish!" she announced, looking around her in triumph, and sailed through the swing doors.

Activities

Reading

1 What was Lorna Sage's secret plan? What was her reason for making it? How well did it succeed?

2 Why would the title *Hurry On Down* remain fixed in Lorna Sage's memory?

3 Do you think that the nurse really knew that Lorna Sage had delayed coming to the hospital? Why did she slap her?

4 How did Lorna Sage feel about her new baby? Try to answer in your own words.

5 Describe some of the rules and regulations in the ward. Why, according to the author, were they so restrictive and unfriendly?

6 What was the attitude of the nurses to:

- mothers
- fathers
- babies?

Discussion

7 How have attitudes to unmarried mothers changed since the extract was written?

8 What about attitudes to older women having babies? Share your ideas with the class.

Language study

9 Look at the following quotation: 'Words like 'delivery' and 'confinement' (threats, promises) hung around in my imagination'.
What do the words 'delivery' and 'confinement' mean in the context of a maternity ward?
In what way can the word 'confinement' be a threat?
In what way can the word 'delivery' be a promise?

10 Look at Lorna Sages's use of brackets in the fourth paragraph of the extract. What kind of information does she include in them? Would the description have worked better if she had included this in the main flow of the writing?

Writing

11 Write a letter from Lorna to her boyfriend Vic from hospital. Describe how you feel about the baby and about being in hospital.

Compare and contrast

12 Compare this account with that of Rachel Cusk on page 84. How are the two descriptions similar? What picture of the medical profession emerges from both of them? Do you think it is a fair picture?

Disappearing Mother

Jenny Diski

JENNY DISKI lost both her parents at about the same time, though not in the usual way.

I last saw my mother on 22 April 1966. You may find my certainty of the date significant, but I remember it because I know the last time I saw her was two days after my father died. The date in my memory is the date of his death.

When I was fourteen, I was admitted, after an overdose, to the mental hospital in Hove where I stayed for four and a half months, stuck, because the psychiatrist in charge wouldn't let me live with either of my parents. My father was in Banbury, my mother in Hove. The mother of a schoolfriend heard about me and offered me a home in her house in London which I, the psychiatrist and both my parents gratefully accepted. When my father died in 1966 I was still living in her house, aged eighteen, and two months away from taking my A-levels.

Two days after my father died, my mother came through the front door and handed me an umbrella. A gift. For April showers and stormy weather. It wasn't any ordinary umbrella, it was pale, powder-blue and shaped like a pagoda, its spire rising to a delicate point, and all around the base was a scalloped frill made of a matching powder-blue, nylon chiffon-like material. Look for the chiffon lining – blue skies, nothing but blue skies – on the sunny side of the street – every time it rains it rains pennies from heaven – come rain or come shine.

I hadn't been in contact with my father for over a year and, apart from a nasty moment over my hospital bed in Hove, my mother hadn't seen him for a lot longer than that. He had died of a heart attack, his second in a few months. After the first attack, Pam, the woman he was living with, had written to my mother asking her to let me know.
She hadn't.

My mother sat down to lunch. She was almost feverishly elated. *She was pleased he was dead. It served him right for being the bastard he was. And she wasn't a hypocrite. She'd always said, hadn't she always said* – she had always said – *that if she saw him lying dead in the gutter she'd kick him out of the way and walk by. And that's what she would do if she saw him now lying in his coffin. She'd spit on him right as he lay there. And laugh. But, as a matter of fact, she didn't think he was really dead, anyway. She thought he was just pretending to be dead, the lying scheming louse that he was, so that he wouldn't have to pay her the £5 a month alimony. She thought ...*

The woman I was living with was present and at this point, thinking I needed something more than a blue umbrella, reminded me about an A-level class I had to get to. I'd better hurry, she said, or I'd miss it. I hurried so much getting out of the house to the non-existent class that I forgot to take any money with me, so I wandered down to Camden High Street and took sanctuary in the library, prepared to give it a couple of hours before my mother ran out of steam and went on her way. The library had a large plate-glass window, and my mother, instead of turning left to the nearest tube and bus stop when she got to the High Street, inexplicably turned right and walked right past the library window. Not actually past. She was already screaming when she pushed through the doors. I sat in silence while she shrieked and wept, noisily enumerating my faults, not the least of which was being just like him: a liar, deceitful, treacherous, heartless. All true, actually, in this context. It provided some dramatic entertainment for the tramps keeping warm, a couple of genuine students and the mothers and children choosing their books for the week, to whom she turned to witness the tragedy of a woman with an unnatural daughter. Then she departed, her aria over, leaving the library in a silence it rarely achieved in the normal course of the day. I watched her disappear past the window in the direction of Camden Town underground, and then, I supposed, back to Hove, after her day out in London. I never saw her again.

My father's death was an extraordinary event, but my mother's dramatics were not, though she had outdone herself being, I had to acknowledge, probably distraught about my father. Usually, after a scene like this, there would be a silence and then she would get in touch again. I wasn't surprised not to hear from her for a while.

My mother's silence continued, and I didn't do anything about it. I didn't want to speak to her, and the fact that she didn't want to speak to me was a relief, putting off the next unpleasantness. The silence elongated into months, then years and then decades. I dumped school just before the exams, moved into a bedsit, sank into depression and began my second period of hospitalization. After eighteen months I had a choice – spend the rest of my life doing the rounds of London bins, or practise real life. I went to teacher training college, became a teacher in a comprehensive school in Hackney, married, changed my name and had my daughter when I was thirty, wrote and published my first novel at thirty-five, wrote more novels. From time to time I'd think about the possibility that my mother would get in touch with me, and a slight panic would flutter through me. I never thought of getting in touch with her.

Activities

Reading

1 In your own words, describe how Jenny Diski came to be living away from both her parents when her father died.

2 Why do you think that Jenny's mother bought the gift of an umbrella?

3 Jenny's mother makes two major speeches in this extract. The first, about her father, is given more or less in her mother's own words. The second, about Jenny, is reported. Why do you think Jenny Diski has done this?

4 What, briefly, were Jenny's mother's feelings about her ex-husband? What did she feel Jenny had in common with her father?

5 Why did the woman Jenny lived with invent an A-level class for her to go to?

6 Why did Jenny not attempt to get in touch with her mother?

Discussion

7 Jenny Diski suffered two major periods of hospitalization as a result of mental illness. Judging from the account, her mother also suffered some form of mental illness. Do you think mental illness is inherited or do you think that the stress of having such a volatile mother might have contributed to the author's own difficulties? Discuss your ideas with the rest of the class.

8 Jenny Diski must have been extremely embarrassed by her mother's appearance in the library. Have your parents ever embarrassed you? Share your experiences in your group.

Language study

9 If you look at Jenny's mother's speech given in italics you will notice that it does not contain exactly the words her mother spoke. How would it need to be changed to do this? What is the effect of reporting her words in this way? Why do you think Jenny Diski interrupts the flow of the speech with the words 'she had always said'.

10 In the sentence beginning, 'I went to teacher training college', the pronoun 'I' is applied to seven verbs. Read the sentence carefully and identify the verbs. What is the effect of attaching so many verbs to one pronoun?

Writing

11 Imagine you were one of the 'genuine students' in the library. Describe what you would have seen and heard when Jenny's mother made her dramatic entrance. Use as many details for your account as possible.

Father and Son

Edmund Gosse

EDMUND GOSSE (1849–1928) grew up in a deeply religious family. His father hoped that Edmund would take up a religious calling when he grew to manhood.

MY Father, then, like an old divine, concentrated on thoughts upon the intellectual part of faith. In his obsession about me, he believed that if my brain could be kept unaffected by any of the seductive errors of the age, and my heart centred in the adoring love of God, all would be well with me in perpetuity.[1] He was still convinced that by intensely directing my thoughts, he could compel them to flow in a certain channel, since he had not begun to learn the lesson, so mournful for saintly men of his complexion, that 'virtue would not be virtue, could it be given by one fellow creature to another'. He had recognized, with reluctance, that holiness was not hereditary, but he continued to hope that it might be compulsive. I was still 'the child of many prayers', and it was not to be conceded that these prayers could remain unanswered.

The great panacea[2] was now, as always, the study of the Bible, and this my Father never ceased to urge upon me. He presented to me a copy of Dean Alford's edition of the Greek New Testament, in four great volumes, and these he had had so magnificently bound in full morocco that the work shone

1 ***in perpetuity:*** for ever
2 ***panacea:*** cure for all problems

on my poor shelf of sixpenny poets like a duchess among dairymaids. He extracted from me a written promise that I would translate and meditate upon a portion of the Greek text every morning before I started for business. This promise I presently failed to keep, my good intentions being undermined by an invincible *ennui*;[3] I concealed the dereliction[4] from him, and the sense that I was deceiving my Father ate into my conscience like a canker. But the dilemma was now before me that I must either deceive my Father in such things or paralyse my own character.

My growing distaste for the Holy Scriptures began to occupy my thoughts, and to surprise as much as it scandalized me. My desire was to continue to delight in those sacred pages, for which I still had an instinctive veneration.[5] Yet I could not but observe the difference between the zeal with which I snatched at a volume of Carlyle[6] or Ruskin[7] – since these magicians were now first revealing themselves to me – and the increasing languor with which I took up Alford for my daily 'passage'. Of course, although I did not know it, and believed my reluctance to be sinful, the real reason why I now found the Bible so difficult to read was my familiarity with its contents. These had the colourless triteness[8] of a story retold a hundred times. I longed for something new, something that would gratify curiosity and excite surprise. Whether the facts and doctrines contained in the Bible were

---

[3] ***ennui:*** boredom
[4] ***dereliction:*** deliberate neglect
[5] ***veneration:*** awe or reverence
[6] ***Carlyle:*** nineteenth-century writer of history and criticism
[7] ***Ruskin:*** nineteenth-century writer on art and morality
[8] ***triteness:*** dullness

true or false was not the question that appealed to me; it was rather that they had been presented to me so often and had sunken into me so far that, as someone has said, they 'lay bedridden in the dormitory of the soul', and made no impression of any kind upon me.

It often amazed me, and I am still unable to understand the fact, that my Father, through his long life – or till nearly the close of it – continued to take an eager pleasure in the text of the Bible. As I think I have already said, before he reached middle life, he had committed practically the whole of it to memory, and if started anywhere, even in a Minor Prophet, he could go on without a break as long as ever he was inclined for that exercise. He, therefore, at no time can have been assailed by the satiety[9] of which I have spoken, and that it came so soon to me I must take simply as an indication of difference of temperament. It was not possible, even through the dark glass of correspondence, to deceive his eagle eye in this matter, and his suspicions accordingly took another turn. He conceived me to have become, or to be becoming, a victim of 'the infidelity of the age'.

In this new difficulty, he appealed to forms of modern literature by the side of which the least attractive pages of Leviticus or Deuteronomy struck me as even thrilling. In particular, he urged upon me a work, then just published, called *The Continuity of Scripture* by William Page Wood, afterwards Lord Chancellor Hatherley. I do not know why he supposed that the lucubrations[10] of an exemplary lawyer, delivered in a style that was like the trickling of sawdust, would succeed in rousing emotions which the glorious

9 ***satiety:*** being full up to the point of disgust or boredom
10 ***lucubrations:*** tiring studies, especially carried out at night

rhetoric of the Orient had failed to awaken; but Page Wood had been a Sunday School teacher for thirty years, and my Father was always unduly impressed by the acumen of pious barristers.

As time went on, and I grew older and more independent in mind, my Father's anxiety about what he called 'the pitfalls and snares which surround on every hand the thoughtless giddy youth of London' became extremely painful to himself. By harping in private upon these 'pitfalls' – which brought to my imagination a funny rough woodcut in an old edition of Bunyan,[11] where a devil was seen capering over a sort of box let neatly into the ground – he worked himself up into a frame of mind which was not a little irritating to his hapless correspondent, who was now 'snared' indeed, limed[12] by the pen like a bird by the feet, and could not by any means escape. To a peck or a flutter from the bird the implacable fowler would reply:

> You charge me with being suspicious, and I fear I cannot deny the charge. But I can appeal to your own sensitive and thoughtful mind for a considerable allowance. My deep and tender love for you; your youth and inexperience; the examples of other young men; your distance from parental counsel; our absolute and painful ignorance of all the details of your daily life, except what you yourself tell us: – try to throw yourself into the standing of a parent, and say if my suspiciousness is unreasonable. I rejoicingly acknowledge that from all I see you are pursuing a virtuous, steady, worthy course. One good thing my suspiciousness does: – ever and

[11] ***Bunyan:*** author of *Pilgrim's Progress*, a very popular Christian book
[12] ***limed:*** trapped

> anon it brings out from you assurances, which greatly refresh and comfort me. And again, it carries me ever to God's Throne of Grace on your behalf. Holy Job *suspected* that his sons might have sinned, and cursed God in their heart. Was not his suspicion much like mine, grounded on the same reasons and productive of the same results? For it drove him to God in intercession. I have adduced the example of this Patriarch before, and he will endure being looked at again.

In fact, Holy Job continued to be frequently looked at, and for this Patriarch I came to experience a hatred which was as venomous as it was undeserved. But what youth of eighteen would willingly be compared with the sons of Job? And indeed, for my part, I felt much more like that justly exasperated character, Elihu the Buzite,[13] of the kindred of Ram.

As time went on, the peculiar strain of inquisition was relaxed, and I endured fewer and fewer of the torments of religious correspondence. Nothing abides in one tense projection, and my Father, resolute as he was, had other preoccupations. His orchids, his microscope, his physiological researches, his interpretations of prophecy, filled up the hours of his active and strenuous life, and, out of his sight, I became not indeed out of his mind, but no longer ceaselessly in the painful foreground of it. Yet, although the reiteration of his anxiety might weary him a little as it had wearied me well nigh to groans of despair, there was not the slightest change in his real attitude towards the subject or towards me.

[13] ***Elihu the Buzite:*** a person who, in the story of Job in the Bible, became angry at the lack of wisdom of his elders

Activities

Reading

1 How did Edmund Gosse's father hope to ensure that his son would follow a religious calling?

2 What was the result as far as Edmund Gosse was concerned?

3 How did Edmund Gosse's attitude to the Bible differ from that of his father?

4 Why do you think Gosse's father thought that translating a passage of the Bible from Greek would be better for his son than a simple reading?

5 Why do you think the passage includes such a long quotation from the father's letter? What does it tell us about him?

6 Why did the writer's father eventually stop nagging him?

Discussion

7 Do you think Edmund Gosse's father was right to be so insistent on his son's religious life? Do you think that the father's obsession contributed to the son's lack of enthusiasm?

8 Do you know any other examples of this kind of behaviour, for instance a father trying to pass on his love of a sport? Do you think fathers have the right to force their ideas and enthusiasms on to their children? Is religion different? Share your experiences and opinions with the class.

Language study

9 Edmund Gosse employs a number of striking similes using 'like' in this text. Identify these and comment on the two or three you think work best.

Writing

10 Write a letter to an advice column in a newspaper in which Edmund Gosse explains his problems with his father. You can then write a reply, which should be as sensitive as possible to the feelings of both father and son.

Compare and contrast

11 Which is worse – a parent who neglects his or her children or one who smothers them in concern? Discuss these ideas using evidence from the accounts by Edmund Gosse and Jenny Diski (page 93).

School

The impact of school on our lives is unpredictable. Sometimes the people are important; sometimes what is studied has a profound effect; sometimes the place where schooling happens is crucial. The accounts in this section look at schools in Wales, Ireland and Italy and demonstrate some of the variety of school experiences.

A Welsh Childhood

Alice Thomas Ellis

AN eye for detail and some vivid images distinguish Alice Thomas Ellis's memories of school.

I went to the National School on the coast road and, since Penmaenmawr slopes as it does, my first classroom was half underground. In the winter it was warmed by an open stove and we did our sums on wood-framed slates using slate pencils which, licked and held in a certain way, made the sort of noise that drives some people mad – like a long fingernail scratching a nylon stocking. Certain of my friends, having discovered the power of this noise, would slide the last part of the road to school down the slate-lined gutters with a granite chipping under foot.

I had enemies too. There was a boy called Robert who lived in Penmaenan (all our enemies lived in Penmaenan, which was out of bounds except for raiding parties) who had thick glasses and a chronic dribble, and used to chase me round the playground. He caught me and kissed me one day, and I was reprimanded by the headmaster, who said he would never have expected such a thing of me. I have never recovered from the injustice of this and I hope Robert has had a rotten life. Then there was a little English boy whose name I never knew, who didn't even attempt to fraternize with the natives but played trains all by himself, going *choo choo* and working his elbows like pistons. The badder boys jeered at him in the playground and he once made a response so dignified and so touching that I wept. I can't remember what it was, but the memory still brings tears to my eyes. I dare say today I should want to smack him.

As time went by our teacher, G.O. Jones, taught us, among other things, to write properly, with a pen. This involved penholders and nibs and wipers and ink monitors whose duty it was to refill the inkwells on each desk, which must have been quite tricky since most of us used them as receptacles for the cod-liver oil capsules and iron pills which a caring authority deemed necessary for our health. G.O. had been gassed in the First World War and as a result he spat a bit as he spoke, and our exercise books came up in moisture bubbles when he stood beside us. He, too, had trouble with Robert whose mother used to burst in roaring when her boy had been quite correctly caned. G.O. said she was a *blackguard* and I admired this sophisticated choice of words, although I wouldn't have cared to cross her myself.

Activities

Reading

1 How did different people react to the noise that can be produced by scraping along slate?

2 Why was Alice Thomas Ellis so angry about being told off?

3 What was eccentric about the English boy that Alice Thomas Ellis remembers?

4 Do you find it odd that she can remember that he once made a very dignified reply but not what he said? Do you have similar 'gaps' in your memory?

5 What did the students put in their inkwells? What does this show about their attitude to health initiatives?

6 What were G.O. Jones's advantages and disadvantages as a teacher?

Discussion

7 Are there any students you have lost touch with since your primary school? What do you remember about them particularly? Share your thoughts with a partner or in a small group.

8 In a group, discuss how your oral anecdotes differ from written narratives. What is gained or lost in an oral narrative?

9 What groups are mentioned in this extract? What groups of students were there at your primary school?

Language study

10 Alice Thomas Ellis admired her teacher's use of the term 'blackguard' to describe a parent. Even when Alice Thomas Ellis was writing this was an old-fashioned term. Why do you think insulting terms go out-of-date so quickly? You can give examples from your own experience if they are not too rude.

Writing

11 Write a description of a student you remember from primary school. Mention how they behaved as well as what they looked like.

An Italian Education

Tim Parks

SENDING his son to school in Italy caused Tim Parks to recall his own schooling in England and draw some interesting comparisons.

WHEN I went to primary school, I carried no bag, because the books were all there, inside my desk. Or if I did, it was a pump bag for gym, or for games. Later, when there was homework, one carried a little briefcase, which went with the collar and tie – we were little businessmen, little accountants and executives, travelling to school on bus and tube – and inside that bag it smelled of sandwiches because the school meals were so awful you opted out.

In Italian schools only essential texts are provided and only up to a certain age. Others are bought by the parents. They're expensive. This means that if they were left in the school, people would be afraid of their being stolen, afraid of having to pay for them again, afraid of losing all the places they have underlined them and written notes in the margin. There are no lockers.

So the children carry all their books to school every day – from six years old to eighteen. Not in briefcases, which probably wouldn't be big enough and certainly wouldn't go with the casual clothing the children wear. Instead, they have backpacks of fluorescent pink and yellow with 'Invicta' written on them and shiny plastic buckles, the same as they will carry years later about the streets of

Rome and Paris and London when their mothers finally feel able to let them go away for a few days on a school journey. I weighed Michele's school backpack one morning. Five kilos of books ...

But however heavy they may be, their backpacks will never smell of sandwiches, because the food is so good no one would ever dream of opting out of school meals. Or rather, the mothers would never dream of letting the authorities let the food get so bad that anyone would want to opt out.

And they'll never smell of football boots either. For school offers no games, no extracurricular activities. There are no music lessons, no singing lessons, no school choir, no carpentry for the boys and cookery for the girls, no hockey, no cricket, no netball, no basketball, no football, no swimming, no athletics, no sports day, no school teams. The school doesn't, as it does in England, pretend to offer a community that might in any way supplant the family, or rival Mamma. That's important. It doesn't, and later on the university won't either, try to create in the child the impression of belonging to a large social unit with its own identity. There is no assembly in the morning, no hymn singing, no prayers, no speech day. Apart from the centenary, which, as the headmistress pointed out, can hardly happen every day, school, for Stefi at six, for Michele at eight, is no more and no less than reading and writing and mathematics, geography and science, oh, and English (just introduced) and, of course, *l'ora di religione*,[1] or, in my children's case, 'Osservazione all'Europa',[2] where

[1] ***l'ora di religione:*** religious education
[2] ***Osservazione all'Europa:*** European education

they have now learned that one of the things that unites European nations is, not our school, not our state, but our ... religion.

The Reformation[3] can wait.

No, if children want extracurricular activity of any kind, they have to go outside school; the parents have to look for it, and take them there ... and pay. Late afternoons become full of *sacrifici*[4] of time and money.

When I was a child, to play football we headed for the nearest public park or waste ground after school and kicked the ball at each other. Or we played with a tennis ball in the playground. Sometimes there would be two or three games of different age groups all crossing each other, up and down, right to left on the bumpy tarmac. On games afternoons the Maths teacher or the R.I. teacher would split us into eleven against eleven, or however many we happened to be, and let us loose on the playing fields. Playing, we learned to play, and I seem to remember having a good time, too. But apparently this was wrong. Or so the young fellow who takes the inscriptions at A.C. Montecchio tells me. Apparently, this was terribly ingenuous[5] of us and explains why English football is now so backward. No, no, no, they take their sport much more seriously, he assures me, in Italy. Or perhaps it's just the times that have changed.

---

3 ***The Reformation:*** the period when Catholic Christianity was challenged and, in many countries replaced, by Protestant Christianity. Italy is still a mainly Catholic country. The United Kingdom is mainly Protestant.

4 ***sacrifici:*** sacrifices

5 ***ingenuous:*** innocent or naïve

In any event, there are no playing fields at the primary school, or the *scuola media*,[6] the next one up, and there are no public spaces here where kids can just play. To play football on grass your kid has to enroll in A.C. Montecchio ...

You take your boy along to the village's only field, surrounded by a cypress hedge and tall fences and a gate to lock it up when it's not being used officially. That's an important concept. You pay up. Not much. Your son is given a kit bag in the team's colour with the name of the team on the side, a team shirt and team shorts. A.C. Montecchio has a new coach this year, a man, incredibly, who used to play for the Hungarian national side, or so the big posters they've put out around the village claim. But this celebrity only teaches the older teams. Then his wisdom is passed down through team members to the infant groups. And what it mainly involves is drilling. Because it's not worth starting to play football until you have done hours of drilling, hours upon hours, just as there's no point in playing the piano until you've done all your scales, major and minor, backwards and forwards.

You go to pick the boy up at five-thirty perhaps on an October evening. It's deep twilight, and they're still running about touching their toes and jumping in the air, then practising penalties, then practising headers. At the end there's only time for a ten-minute game, under the dim glare of one of four floodlights now. By December, whoever's in goal freezes to death, though he does have the official team gloves. The trainer screams and shrieks for the kids to pass. "Pass, *per l'amore di Dio*![7] The way I told you in

[6] ***scuola media:*** middle school
[7] ***per l'amore di Dio:*** for the love of God

the drill!" He blows his whistle a lot, though rarely for fouls. He sends one boy off for holding onto the ball too long. Then he sends another off for saying *porca vacca!*[8] Good job it wasn't Michele.

Training's supposed to end at six, but drags on and on. They want us to know that they take it very, very seriously and are developing our children's talents. These pieties are in the air, which otherwise is icy now. Frankly, I'm shivering. In fact, I'm savouring the word *sacrifici*, rolling it over and over on my tongue, while from the touchline other waiting parents are yelling complicated advice into the gloom. "*Devi gestire lo spazio in modo dinamico!*" You have to have a dynamic sense of territorial control! Little Mirko doesn't even look up, idling in an offside position. The parents wave their arms. Generally, both mothers and fathers are disappointed with their sons' performances. They shout things even worse than *porca vacca*. Why can't the kids do it like on TV? God knows they watch enough! Michele gets the ball full and hard in his face and keels over on the frosty grass.

The gate to the pitch is at the end of Zia Natalina's street and going back we pick up Stefi, who is inside in the warm learning to cut pieces of folded paper so that they will come out as angels with joined hands. "*Santa patata*,[9] Michele," Zia says, "you look like the abominable snowman." Actually, his face is bright red. Very soon he will decide he doesn't like football.

[8] ***porca vacca***: a mild insult
[9] ***santa patata***: holy potato (an exclamation of mild surprise)

Activities

Reading

1 What is the main difference in textbook provision between Italy and the England of Tim Parks' youth? Are your own experiences of school bags closer to Tim Parks or to those of Italian children?

2 Why do Italian children never opt out of school meals? Who assures the quality of school meals in Italy?

3 According to Tim Parks, schools in England form an alternative community. Why do they do not do this in Italy?

4 What was Tim Park's attitude to playing football when he was at school? How does this differ from the Italian attitude?

5 Why do you think Michele will soon decide he doesn't like football?

Discussion

6 Tim Parks seems to suggest that mothers and their opinions are very important in Italy. Does he approve of this? How can you tell? Discuss the passage in small groups and be prepared to report your findings to the rest of the class.

7 Based on this passage, would you prefer to be educated in Italy or in England? Give reasons for your opinions.

Language study

8 Look at Tim Parks' use of lists in the paragraph beginning, 'But however heavy they may be'. How does the format of these lists reveal his bias in favour of the English way of doing things?

9 Why is the sentence 'The Reformation can wait' given a paragraph to itself?

Writing

10 Interview an adult about his or her school days and write a report on how schooling has changed since your interviewee was at school. If you have language assistants at your school, you could also interview one of them about how schooling is different in their country of origin.

Compare and contrast

11 Two of the extracts in this section are autobiographical and one is by an adult commenting on his children's schooling. Which of the three extracts gives you the best idea of what it is like to be in school? Which aspects of the text, such as information or description, help you to form an impression?

At School in Ireland

Edna O'Brien

ALTHOUGH Edna O'Brien recalls many physical details of her schooldays, the part she seems to relish most is the introduction to the world of stories that school provided.

WHEN it rained and the yard was too wet for playtime, we huddled in the porch – forty or fifty girls – like hens except that we were chattering, huddled next to the reek of turf.[1] Turf can gel into one's head, making thoughts brown and sodden and flaky as the stuff itself. We would eat lunch there. Everyone's lunch much the same – thick slices of bread and butter, with sugar sprinkled on some, and a little bottle of water or milk. Our coats would be on hooks, coats slung on top of one another all threatening to fall off, then pixie caps of multifarious orders, scarfs and wool gloves that had been chewed and re-chewed and were anything but pristine.

Your best jumper was from a knitting pattern, little diamonds of colour, zig-zags, the cynosure[2] of all. You were called in by your teacher on an important occasion for it to be inspected by someone. By whom? You have forgotten. Forgotten everything except the beautiful waves of colour, and the zip with the flecked tassle at the end, and the ribbed cuffs of navy wool, that doubled over twice in case you should grow. You wore it Sundays, Holy Days and the

1 ***turf:*** dried turf can be used as fuel
2 ***cynosure:*** way it attracts attention to its beauty

days inspectors came. You told the catechism[3] inspector that after the miracle of the loaves and fishes, when all had eaten to their satisfaction, Christ asked them to gather up the remains and that proved that He was not partial to waste.

The fishes in your imagination were flesh pink, medium sized like dab, and the loaves were white like altar breads, only fatter and spongier. The place where the miracle occurred was green and leafy and not at all the sparse sanded land that you were later to see. After the inspector went you all got a telling off, were told you could sweep the countryside with your brains except that instead you all chose to be bostoons. The only girls who did not get a telling off were the ones who were permanently dense and from whom nothing was expected beyond the norm. On that day they were the proud ones with their arms folded, and something verging on compliments descending on them because of the neatness of their appearance, or because they knew when to close the door or put a sod on the fire.

It was all very unpredictable. The teacher could flare up, have fits, pet some girls on the backs of their knees, have sets on other girls, then mysteriously change her mind and applaud those she was previously denigrating. But when the boys' master got into a tear it was bedlam for everyone. He roared and shouted and any adjacent boy was in danger of having his brains bashed out, onto the desk. He could be heard a mile away, roaring at whatever unfortunate boy was his butt. It was a constant threat like living close to

[3] ***catechism:*** a collection of questions and answers on matters of faith

Mount Vesuvius.[4] His wife prayed, said constant ejaculations,[5] and told women on the way down from Mass that he had not realized his ambition. He did the crosswords, had greyhounds that were fidgety and as a consequence the woodwork in their rambling house had the teeth marks of baying dissatisfied dogs.

Monday mornings were especially tense – compositions were handed over or not handed over, lies were told, how a mother or a father had been taken sick and the school fire was in no mind to light not having been lit for two whole days. The compositions were usually about 'A Day in the Life of a Penny' or 'A Day in the Life of a King' or 'A Day in the Life of a Bee' and we had to do lessons while she sat down to correct them and laughed outrageously at the clumsiness of our thoughts and our ideas. With a ruler as a pointer one girl would trace the course of the river, most often the River Shannon, with its important tributary, the Suck, and in the corner of our eyes we imagined the mice's tails as they curled above the level of the holes, or stared at the jam jars of lilac that had been brought in by one of the country girls and had withered on the window ledge so that specks of petal were lying like bits of must there and the water in the jar would have gone off.

Another world altogether sometimes prevailed – one of arms crests, spears, Lughaidh Laeighseach, son of Laeigh, son of the renowned Conall Cearnach. chief of the Red Branch Knights of Ulster, unbecomingly slain by a tribe which was later brutally avenged. Or a poem about Owen Roe O'Neill, 'Him they poisoned whom they feared to meet

4 ***Mount Vesuvius:*** a volcano
5 ***ejaculations:*** short prayers

with steel', or a description of Shane O'Neill's body dug up at Carrickfergus, the head cut off and dispatched to Dublin where it was exhibited on the castle battlements. Shane O'Neill was a tough man because upon being told that they had murdered his only son he had replied that he had many sons. These daily inculcations of history, so immediate, so heartrending and so riveting that it was possible to conceive of Sarsfield, Shane O'Neill and Bold Robert Emmet, and Sarah Curran his sweetheart, as characters who might step out of the pages and into the room. All had sacrificed themselves for the Cause, and each had failed – one went into lowly exile, the other had his head on the castle battlement, the third was executed in the Liberties and made a speech from the dock that wrung our hearts – how his blood was not congealed by artificial terrors, and that though the lamp of his life was nearly extinguished he was ready to die and asked only for the charity of silence until such time as his country was free and not annexed to England.

Fair Sarah Curran went abroad, married and of course died of a broken heart. To Theobald Wolfe Tone, too, honour cursed with defeat. In 1796 with a hundred guineas in his pocket he went to Paris to secure a large force to help overthrow the British government in Ireland. The Bantry Bay expedition was the result of that, and Tone sailed for Ireland with an army of fifteen thousand men under the command of General Hoche and General Grouchy. His account of that voyage was like a letter from a son to each one of us.

> The wind is still high, and as usual right ahead; and I dread a visit from the English; and altogether I am in great uneasiness. Oh, that we were once ashore, let what might ensue after; I am sick to the very soul of this suspense ... We are here, sixteen sail, great and small, scattered up and down in a noble bay, and so dispersed that the enemy are now so close that if it blows tonight as it did last night they will inevitably run foul of each other, unless one of them prefers driving on the shore.

Then the bitter tail-piece – three ships sunk, the others parted from each other, a difference of opinion with Grouchy and such storms as made Tone fear that it was his fate to submit and turn back to France. Two years later he led another fleet which was dismantled, captured by the British and led into Lough Swilly. Tone was taken prisoner. As the gallows was being erected outside his window, he cut his throat with a penknife but did not die at once and said to the surgeon that it was a pity he had been such a bad anatomist.

One had only to look out the long window and imagine the masts, the rigging, the ribs, the rudders and the sails appearing over the bottle-topped walls. The sea was 40 miles away and, as we were told, withheld at one side by shining sheer gigantic black cliffs, from whence a priest was sucked in one afternoon, while doing a spot of fishing. Conjecture as to whether he could have given himself absolution or even uttered an act of contrition as he hurtled forward and downwards in the wake of the bamboo fishing rod that he'd bought in the hardware shop the day before. The sea spelled catastrophe but then all waters did, even the lordly Shannon into which cars had driven, or boats were overturned or men delivered up their own lives. The Shannon lake shone in summer and was hazed over with a special fly in the month of May, a fly for fishing with, for dapping. Lough Dearg Deire – the Lake of the King of the Red Eye, so named because an unreasonable grasping bard had asked the King of Thomand for an eye, whereupon the King plucked out his own, gave it over, went down to the lake to wash, but his socket bled until the lake was not water but human blood.

Activities

Reading

1 Why do you think Edna O'Brien remembers her 'best jumper' so vividly?
2 What went wrong for the clever students on the day the catechism inspector came?
3 How did the girls' teacher treat her pupils?
4 How did the boys' teacher treat his pupils? What explanation did his wife give for his behaviour?
5 What do most of the stories that Edna O'Brien enjoyed from Irish literature and history have in common?
6 How does Edna O'Brien see the landscape? Is she more interested in what it looks like or in what happened there?

Discussion

7 Edna O'Brien gained a strong sense of Irish history from her time at primary school. Which subjects fired your imagination most at primary school?
8 Were any of your primary school teachers as memorable as the ones Edna O'Brien encountered? Share your memories in pairs or small groups.

Language study

9 This passage begins and ends using 'we', but a long section uses 'you' as the main pronoun. What is the purpose of this shift? How does Edna O'Brien's referring to herself as 'you' help to involve the audience?
10 Some of Edna O'Brien's memories are very vivid, whilst others are vague. How does she indicate the vagueness of some of the details of her memory in the second paragraph? Do you think being so honest is a good idea? Why?

Writing

11 Attempt a composition or short, descriptive essay entitled 'A Day in the Life of a Penny'.
12 Write a description of a day at your primary school. Choose a particular day that stands out in your memory.

Places

Writing from a personal point of view provides us with a means of travelling in both space and time. The extracts in this section will take you back to the nineteenth century.

Daffodils

Dorothy Wordsworth

DOROTHY WORDSWORTH (1771–1855) was the devoted sister of the poet William Wordsworth. She shared his love of nature and often joined her brother on his walks around the Lake District.

Thursday, 15 April 1802

It was a threatening misty morning – but mild. We set off after dinner from Eusemere. Mrs Clarkson went a short way with us but turned back. The wind was furious and we thought we must have returned. We first rested in the large Boat-house, then under a furze Bush opposite Mr Clarkson's. Saw the plough going in the field. The wind seized our breath, the Lake was rough. There was a Boat by itself floating in the middle of the Bay below Water Millock. We rested again in the Water Millock Lane. The hawthorns are black and green, the birches here and there greenish but there is yet more of purple to be seen on the Twigs. We got over into a field to avoid some cows – people working, a few primroses by the roadside, woodsorrel flower, the anemone, scentless violets, strawberries, and that starry yellow flower which Mrs C. calls pilewort. When we were in the woods beyond Gowbarrow Park we saw a few daffodils close to the water side. We fancied that the lake had floated the seeds ashore and that the little colony had so sprung up. But as we went along there were more and yet more and at last under the boughs of the trees, we saw that there was a long belt of them along the shore, about the breadth of a country turnpike road. I never saw daffodils so beautiful; they grew among the mossy stones about and about them, some rested their heads upon these stones as on a pillow for weariness and the rest tossed and reeled and danced and seemed as if they verily laughed with the wind that blew upon them over the lake, they looked so gay, ever glancing, ever changing. This wind blew directly over the lake to them. There was here and there a little knot and a few stragglers a few yards higher up but they were so few as not to disturb the simplicity and unity of life of that one busy highway. We rested again and again. The Bays were stormy, and we heard the waves at different distances and in the middle of the water like the sea.

Rain came on – we were wet when we reached Luffs but we called in. Luckily all was cheerless and gloomy so we faced the storm – we *must* have been wet if we had waited – put on dry clothes at Dobson's. I was very kindly treated by a young woman, the Landlady looked sour but it is her way. She gave us a goodish supper. Excellent ham and potatoes. We paid 7/–[1] when we came away. William was sitting by a bright fire when I came downstairs. He soon made his way to the Library piled up in a corner of the window. He brought out a volume of Enfield's *Speaker*, another miscellany, and an odd volume of Congreve's plays. We had a glass of warm rum and water. We enjoyed ourselves and wished for Mary. It rained and blew when we went to bed.

NB Deer in Gowbarrow Park like skeletons.

---

[1] ***7/–:*** seven shillings (about 35p) and quite expensive in 1802

I Wandered Lonely as a Cloud

William Wordsworth

THIS is the poem that William Wordsworth (1770–1850) composed on his walk with Dorothy.

I wandered lonely as a cloud
That floats on high o'er vales and hills,
When all at once I saw a crowd,
A host, of golden daffodils;
Beside the lake, beneath the trees,
Fluttering and dancing in the breeze.

Continuous as the stars that shine
And twinkle on the milky way,
They stretched in never-ending line
Along the margin of a bay:
Ten thousand saw I at a glance,
Tossing their heads in sprightly dance.

The waves beside them danced; but they
Out-did the sparkling waves in glee:
A poet could not but be gay,
In such a jocund[1] company:
I gazed – and gazed – but little thought
What wealth the show to me had brought:

[1] ***jocund:*** happy

For oft, when on my couch I lie
In vacant or in pensive[2] mood,
They flash upon that inward eye
Which is the bliss of solitude;
And then my heart with pleasure fills,
And dances with the daffodils.

[2] ***pensive:*** thoughtful

Activities

Reading

1 What details of the landscape in 'Daffodils' seem to interest Dorothy Wordsworth?

2 Apart from the encounter with the daffodils, what was the walk like generally?

3 What impression does William Wordsworth give of the walk he was on in 'I Wandered Lonely as a Cloud'?

4 What was the value to Wordsworth of the encounter with the daffodils according to the final stanza of the poem?

Compare and contrast

5 What features of the bed of daffodils do both Dorothy and William describe?

6 Which of the two descriptions gives you the best impression of the scene? Give reasons for your answer.

7 Which of the two accounts do you prefer? Why?

Discussion

8 Why do you think William Wordsworth edited his sister out of his description of the daffodils? Would the poem have been better if it had included her? Or more truthful?

9 Discuss what the differences between Dorothy and William's accounts tell us about the difference between poetry and a journal. Report your ideas back to the class.

Language study

10 What features of Dorothy's journal suggest that it was not intended for publication? Look at such things as her punctuation and the organization of the account.

Writing

11 Write a brief account of the characters of William and Dorothy Wordsworth based on the evidence of these pieces of writing.

Lark Rise

Flora Thompson

FLORA THOMPSON (1876–1947) grew up in a small village towards the end of the nineteenth century. Her childhood memories recall a time, before motor cars and easy transportation, when English villages were more like small islands than part of a single country.

A few of the houses had thatched roofs, whitewashed outer walls and diamond-paned windows, but the majority were just stone or brick boxes with blue-slated roofs. The older houses were relics of pre-enclosure[1] days and were still occupied by descendants of the original squatters, themselves at that time elderly people. One old couple owned a donkey and cart, which they used to carry their vegetables, eggs, and honey to the market town and sometimes hired out at sixpence[2] a day to their neighbours. One house was occupied by a retired farm bailiff, who was reported to have "well feathered his own nest" during his years of stewardship. Another aged man owned and worked upon about an acre of land. These, the innkeeper, and one other man, a stonemason who walked the three miles to and from his work in the town every day, were the only ones not employed as agricultural labourers.

---

[1] ***pre-enclosure:*** before the common land was fenced to make private farms early in the nineteenth century
[2] ***sixpence:*** two and a half new pence

Some of the cottages had two bedrooms, others only one, in which case it had to be divided by a screen or curtain to accommodate parents and children. Often the big boys of a family slept downstairs, or were put out to sleep in the second bedroom of an elderly couple whose own children were out in the world. Except at holiday times, there were no big girls to provide for, as they were all out in service.[3] Still, it was often a tight fit, for children swarmed, eight, ten, or even more in some families, and although they were seldom all at home together, the eldest often being married before the youngest was born, beds and shakedowns[4] were often so closely packed that the inmates had to climb over one bed to get into another.

But Lark Rise must not be thought of as a slum set down in the country. The inhabitants lived an open-air life; the cottages were kept clean by much scrubbing with soap and water, and doors and windows stood wide open when the weather permitted. When the wind cut across the flat land to the east, or came roaring down from the north, doors and windows had to be closed; but then, as the hamlet people said, they got more than enough fresh air through the keyhole.

There were two epidemics of measles during the decade, and two men had accidents in the harvest field and were taken to hospital; but, for years together, the doctor was only seen there when one of the ancients was dying of old age, or some difficult first confinement baffled the skill of the old woman who, as she said, saw the beginning and end of everybody. There was no cripple or mental defective in

[3] ***in service:*** working as maids or other servants in larger houses
[4] ***shakedowns:*** temporary beds

the hamlet, and, except for a few months when a poor woman was dying of cancer, no invalid. Though food was rough and teeth were neglected, indigestion was unknown, while nervous troubles, there as elsewhere, had yet to be invented. The very word 'nerve' was used in a different sense to the modern one. "My word! An' 'aven't she got a nerve!" they would say of any one who expected more than was reasonable.

In nearly all the cottages there was but one room downstairs, and many of these were poor and bare, with only a table and a few chairs and stools for furniture and a superannuated[5] potato sack thrown down by way of hearthrug. Other rooms were bright and cosy, with dressers of crockery, cushioned chairs, pictures on the walls and brightly coloured hand-made rag rugs on the floor. In these there would be pots of geraniums, fuchsias, and old-fashioned sweet-smelling musk on the windowsills. In the older cottages there were grandfathers' clocks, gate-legged tables, and rows of pewter, relics of a time when life was easier for country folk.

The interiors varied, according to the number of mouths to be fed and the thrift and skill of the housewife, or the lack of those qualities; but the income in all was precisely the same, for ten shillings[6] a week was the standard wage of the farm labourer at that time in that district.

Looking at the hamlet from a distance, one house would have been seen, a little apart, and turning its back on its neighbours, as though about to run away into the fields. It was a small grey stone cottage with a thatched roof, a

5 ***superannuated:*** too old to be of any other use
6 ***ten shillings:*** about 50p

green-painted door and a plum tree trained up the wall to the eaves. This was called the 'end house' and was the home of the stonemason and his family. At the beginning of the decade there were two children: Laura, aged three, and Edmund, a year and a half younger. In some respects these children, while small, were more fortunate than their neighbours. Their father earned a little more money than the labourers. Their mother had been a children's nurse and they were well looked after. They were taught good manners and taken for walks, milk was bought for them, and they were bathed regularly on Saturday nights and, after 'Gentle Jesus' was said, were tucked up in bed with a peppermint or clove ball to suck. They had tidier clothes, too, for their mother had taste and skill with her needle and better-off relations sent them parcels of outgrown clothes. The other children used to tease the little girl about the lace on her drawers and led her such a life that she once took them off and hid them in a haystack.

Their mother at that time used to say that she dreaded the day when they would have to go to school; children got so wild and rude and tore their clothes to shreds going the mile and a half backwards and forwards. But when the time came for them to go she was glad, for, after a break of five years, more babies had begun to arrive, and, by the end of the 'eighties, there were six children at the end house.

As they grew, the two elder children would ask questions of anybody and everybody willing or unwilling to answer them.

Who planted the buttercups? Why did God let the wheat get blighted? Who lived in this house before we did, and what were their children's names? What's the sea like? Is it bigger than Cottisloe Pond? *Why* can't we go to Heaven in the donkey-cart? Is it farther than Banbury? And so on, taking their bearings in that small corner of the world they had somehow got into.

This asking of questions teased their mother and made them unpopular with the neighbours. "Little children should be seen and not heard," they were told at home. Out of doors it would more often be "Ask no questions and you'll be told no lies." One old woman once handed the little girl a leaf from a pot-plant on her window-sill. "What's it called?" was the inevitable question. " 'Tis called mind your own business," was the reply; "an' I think I'd better give a slip of it to your mother to plant in a pot for you." But no such reproofs could cure them of the habit, although they soon learned who and who not to question.

In this way they learned the little that was known of the past of the hamlet and of places beyond. They had no need to ask the names of the birds, flowers, and trees they saw every day, for they had already learned these unconsciously, and neither could remember a time when they did not know an oak from an ash, wheat from barley, or a Jenny wren from a blue-tit. Of what was going on around them, not much was hidden, for the gossips talked freely before children, evidently considering them not meant to hear as well as not to be heard, and, as every house was open to them and their own home was open to most people, there was not much that escaped their sharp ears.

Activities

Reading

1 What evidence does Flora Thompson present that the Lark Rise was a healthy place to live?
2 Why would similar housing in towns be unhealthy?
3 What advantages did Laura and Edmund have over most of the children in the village?
4 What was the attitude of most village people to the children's curiosity?
5 What kind of things did they learn unconsciously?
6 Why did the children have access to so much information about their neighbours?

Discussion

7 Compare your own home to that of Edmund and Laura. What do you have that they didn't have? Would you care to swap places with them? Share your ideas with a partner or in a small group.
8 Why do you think Flora Thompson has chosen to write about herself in the third person? What are the advantages and disadvantages of writing in this manner? Discuss this topic in small groups and be prepared to report back to the class.

Language study

9 Reread the passage and compare its tone before and after the introduction of Laura and Edmund. How does the writing change between the two sections?

Writing

10 Write about yourself in the third person. You can write about yourself as you are now or when you were a child. When you have completed your piece, discuss with a partner whether you found writing in this manner easier or more difficult than writing in the first person.

Compare and contrast

11 All of the extracts in this section describe life in the nineteenth century. Which one gives you the most vivid impression of another time and place? Explain your choice by referring to the details that you find most striking.

Iron Country

William Cobbett

WILLIAM COBBETT (1762–1835) made a series of rides around England on horseback between the years 1822 and 1826. In the journal he published of his travels he described the end of the old, rural England and the beginnings of the new England that was taking shape as a result of the Industrial Revolution.

ALL the way along from Leeds to Sheffield it is coal and iron, and iron and coal. It was dark before we reached Sheffield; so that we saw the iron furnaces in all the horrible splendour of their everlasting blaze. Nothing can be conceived more grand or more terrific than the yellow waves of fire that incessantly issue from the top of these furnaces, some of which are close by the way-side. Nature has placed the beds of iron and the beds of coal alongside of each other, and art has taught man to make one to operate upon the other, as to turn the iron-stone[1] into liquid matter, which is drained off from the bottom of the furnace, and afterwards moulded into blocks and bars, and all sorts of things. The combustibles are put into the top of the furnace, which stands thirty, forty, or fifty feet up in the air, and the ever-blazing mouth of which is kept supplied with coal and coke and iron-stone from little iron waggons forced up by steam, and brought down again to be refilled. It is a

[1] **iron-stone:** iron ore

surprising thing to behold; and it is impossible to behold it without being convinced that, whatever other nations may do with cotton and with wool, they will never equal England with regard to things made of iron and steel.

This Sheffield, and the land all about it, is one bed of iron and coal. They call it black Sheffield, and black enough it is; but from this one town and its environs go nine-tenths of the knives that are used in the whole world; there being, I understand, no knives made at Birmingham; the manufacture of which place consists of the larger sort of implements, of locks of all sorts, and guns and swords, and of all the endless articles of hardware which go to the furnishing of a house. As to the land, viewed in the way of agriculture, it really does appear to be of very little worth. I have not seen, except at Harewood and Ripley, a stack of wheat since I came into Yorkshire; and even there, the whole I saw; and all that I have seen since I came into Yorkshire; and all that I saw during a ride of six miles that I took into Derbyshire the day before yesterday; all put together would not make the one-half of what I have many times seen in one single risk-yard of the vales of Wiltshire. But this is all very proper: these coal-diggers, and iron-melters, and knife-makers, compel us to send the food to them, which, indeed, we do very cheerfully, in exchange for the produce of their rocks, and the wondrous works of their hands.

The trade of Sheffield has fallen off less in proportion than that of the other manufacturing districts. North America, and particularly the United States, where the people have so much victuals[2] to cut, form a great branch of the custom of this town. If the people of Sheffield could only receive a

[2] **victuals:** food

tenth part of what their knives sell for by retail in America, Sheffield might pave its streets with silver. A gross of knives and forks is sold to the Americans for less than three knives and forks can be bought at retail in a country store in America. No fear of rivalship in this trade. The Americans may lay on their tariff, and double it, and triple it; but as long as they continue to cut their victuals, from Sheffield they must have the things to cut it with.

The ragged hills all round about this town are bespangled with groups of houses inhabited by the working cutlers. They have not suffered like the working weavers; for to make knives there must be the hand of man. Therefore, machinery cannot come to destroy the wages of the labourer. The home demand has been very much diminished; but still the depression has here not been what it has been, and what it is where the machinery can be brought into play. We are here just upon the borders of Derbyshire, a nook of which runs up and separates Yorkshire from Nottinghamshire. I went to a village, the day before yesterday, called Mosborough, the whole of the people of which are employed in the making of sickles and scythes and where, as I was told, they are very well off even in the times. A prodigious[3] quantity of these things go to the United States of America. In short, there are about twelve millions of people there continually consuming these things; and the hardware merchants here have their agents and their stores in the great towns of America; which country, as far as relates to this branch of business, is still a part of old England.

---

[3] **prodigious:** very large

Activities

Reading

1 Judging by his description in the first paragraph, how do you think William Cobbett felt about the manufacturing of iron? Give reasons for your answer.

2 What was Cobbett's opinion of the agricultural state of the area around Sheffield?

3 What happens to the price of Sheffield knives when they are exported to America?

4 Why have the knife manufacturers not suffered in the same way as the weavers?

5 What does Cobbett seem most concerned with – the prosperity of the country as a whole or the prosperity of individual groups of workers?

Discussion

6 William Cobbett's observations are about a new technology which caused major changes in society. What new technologies are we adopting today? What kind of changes do you think will take place in such things as patterns of employment and areas of manufacturing? How might your own lives be affected by new technology? Discuss your ideas in a small group and then report back to the class.

Language study

7 Look at the following sentence:

> 'I have not seen, except at Harewood and Ripley, a stack of wheat since I came into Yorkshire; and even there, the whole I saw; and all that I have seen since I came into Yorkshire; and all that I saw during a ride of six miles that I took into Derbyshire the day before yesterday; all put together would not make the one-half of what I have many times seen in one single risk-yard of the vales of Wiltshire.'

Discuss with a partner how it builds up. Do you think this gradual coming to a point makes the final point stronger? Or does the length of the sentence make it confusing?

8 Reread the passage and identify phrases and sentences which express facts and those that express Cobbett's personal opinion. Would the passage have been more or less interesting if Cobbett had expressed fewer opinions?

Writing

9 Write a description of your area as it may be in 200 years' time. What will have changed in the scenery, the ways people work and how you would feel about it? Write as an observer, describing the scene in detail.

People

We read writing from a personal perspective to find out how writers view and respond to the world. In this section, the focus is on how writers view and respond to other people. Here you will find some nineteenth-century gossip as well as some twentieth-century wit and wisdom. If these extracts show anything it is that times change but, on the whole, people don't.

Being a Model

Quentin Crisp

Quentin Crisp is known as a great English eccentric. He made no secret of his homosexuality and suffered a great deal of prejudice as a result. He tried a variety of careers in his youth but the job of being an artist's model gave him the least displeasure.

Posing was the first job I had ever had in which I understood what I was doing. Always until now I had worked or tried to work to a standard other than my own. In commercial art I had always made an effort to draw things so that others would find them appetizing and worth their money. Even in my book I had attempted to describe ideas so that others would find them interesting. For some artists and writers this may not be difficult. They may have tastes they share with the average consumer or the gentle reader. I had so little in common with real people that someone once said to me, "I think I like things better before you've praised them." In these circumstances it was hardly surprising that my drawings and my writings brought me so little success. I decided to set about the job of modelling in the opposite way – to force upon the students the qualities that I felt life drawing ought to possess.

When I had attended the art school in High Wycombe twelve long dark years before, the hours I had most enjoyed were those spent in the life room but, though some of the models had been of a beauty like the sun, hardly any of them had seemed to me to be doing enough. They had stood or sat or lain about like ordinary mortals and not a bit like the figures of Michelangelo.[1] I wanted to change all that. I was an avowed enemy of culture but I admired his work unconditionally.

Of all the paintings from the nude that I ever saw, only his appeared to me to be not merely of living people but of what it is like to be alive. The drawings of Ingres,[2] continually held before the lustreless eyes of students as an example for them to follow, always seemed to me to be seen from outside – to display a lascivious[3] preoccupation with surfaces – with the convexities[4] and concavities[5] of the body. Michelangelo worked from within. He described not the delights of touching or seeing a man but the excitement of being Man. Every stroke he made spoke of the pleasure of exerting, restraining and putting to the utmost use the divine gravity-resisting machine. His work had the opposite quality to the paintings of Rembrandt,[6] into whose canvases the subjects stumble, broken, conscious of their physical faults and begging the beholder for forgiveness.

I was determined to be as Sistine[7] as hell. It was fully in accord with my endeavour to live in the continuous present from head to foot. Unfortunately I was not naturally

---

1 ***Michelangelo:*** Italian Renaissance artist and sculptor (1475–1564)
2 ***Ingres:*** French classical painter, noted for his draughtsmanship (1780–1867)
3 ***lascivious:*** sexually exciting
4 ***convexities:*** bulges
5 ***concavities:*** indentations
6 ***Rembrandt:*** Dutch painter (1606–69), famous for his use of light and shade, and for his sensitive portraits
7 ***Sistine:*** ceiling of the Sistine Chapel in Rome – one of Michelangelo's most famous works

equipped to carry out this mission. I was undersized in all respects except for a pigeon chest and a huge head. When stripped, I looked less like 'Il David'[8] than a plucked chicken that died of myxomatosis.[9] It could hardly have been otherwise. I had lived most of my life by starving and gorging alternately and had never taken any exercise other than walking the streets. However, I twisted and turned, climbed up the walls of life rooms and rolled on their paint-daubed floors morning, nude and night for several days a week for six years.

The students were furious.

I had not foreseen this. I had only anticipated hostility from the staff, thinking of teachers as thin, bespectacled, Gothic[10] creatures hysterically concerned for the reputations of their schools. This turned out to be a false image. Art masters were at great pains to distinguish themselves from other pedagogues.[11] Even in those days they were deliberately jolly. When, with time, even teachers of academic subjects began to relax their forbidding posture, art masters found themselves compelled to resort to a rusticity[12] amounting in some cases to oafishness.

Even those who were embarrassed by my antics remained kind. Unhooking me from the picture-rail, they would say quietly, "All you have to do is to stand as though you were waiting for a bus." What kind of an injunction was that when, at a bus stop, I looked as though I were on the

8 ***Il David:*** a sculpture by Michelangelo representing a 'perfect' man
9 ***myxomatosis:*** a disease fatal to rabbits
10 ***Gothic:*** gloomy
11 ***pedagogues:*** teachers
12 ***rusticity:*** behaviour appropriate to the countryside

dais[13] of some life room? One man, working on the Sickert[14] principle, went so far as to assemble a washstand, a cracked basin and a dim grey towel in the hope of toning me down. As I stepped in among these negligently posed props I asked, "And how do you propose to make me look like home?" The instructor who had gone to all this trouble breathed deeply down his nose. "There you have me," he said.

Aware of this difficulty most teachers simply turned me loose on the class. As I stood *en arabesque*[15] on top of a pillar, Mr McCullough said, "Now draw that. Wings optional." He was secretly filled with a fiendish glee at seeing his pupils struggle with a subject that not even they could take for granted. My poses were so extreme they could not be held long enough to suit a painting session. I worked chiefly in drawing classes. I preferred them. Drawing is a science; painting is just something for the long winter evenings.

More than anything it was the fact that my contortions made their work more difficult that caused the students to manifest such hostility. When I had first seen the boys in their corduroy trousers and the girls in their Hungarian blouses, I had assumed that I would get on all right with them. It had been many years since I had been in a crowd of young people. I had forgotten or had never really known what they were like.

---

[13] ***dais:*** raised platform

[14] ***Sickert:*** British impressionist painter (1860–1942), especially of scenes of ordinary life

[15] ***en arabesque:*** with one leg raised behind and both arms stretched out

The young always have the same problem – how to rebel and conform at the same time. They have now solved this by defying their elders and copying one another. The result to grown-ups is that they seem brutish and stuffy at the same time. The fact that I was eccentric did not prejudice them in my favour. I was peculiar in a manner other than theirs and my naïve enthusiasm merely highlighted the fact that I was a generation older than they. I was a senile delinquent: in their eyes an unforgivable sin.

Towards the end of the war art students became very numerous. Perhaps drawing was a pleasant distraction from the bombs before which some people tended to go to pieces. When peace broke out, their number did not decrease. The Minister of Education ran down to the water's edge and, as our brave boys disembarked, scattered grants to art schools over their heads like confetti. Some fell on men whose art training had been interrupted by their service with His Majesty's Forces; some reached stockbrokers, stevedores, street-walkers and stage-managers. Everyone who could availed himself of the Minister's kindness. The chance to study anything without paying fees, even if it is something that can never be the slightest use, must not be allowed to pass by. In this way the Great Art Rush began.

Activities

Reading

1 What had been wrong with Quentin Crisp's attempts at drawing and writing?

2 What did Quentin Crisp admire about the work of Michelangelo? Why was he unsuitable as a Michelangelo-type model?

3 What reaction had Quentin Crisp expected from the art teachers? How did they actually react?

4 What reaction had he expected from the students? How did they actually react?

5 Why didn't the students like Crisp's eccentric behaviour?

6 Why was there such a demand for Quentin Crisp's services as a model shortly after the Second World War?

Discussion

7 Do you agree with Quentin Crisp's statement that the problem for young people is how to rebel and conform at the same time? Discuss your views with a partner or in a small group.

8 Do you think people are more or less tolerant of eccentric behaviour now than they were in the 1950s? Give reasons for your opinions.

Language study

9 Go through the passage and find examples of Quentin Crisp's use of quotation. Why do you think the words he quotes have stuck in his mind?

10 Most of the negative comments in this passage are directed at Quentin Crisp himself. Find two or three examples of this 'self deprecating' humour and explain why they are amusing.

Writing

11 Quentin Crisp occasionally alters well-known clichés to obtain a humorous effect, for instance, 'morning, nude and night' and 'senile delinquent'. Brainstorm a list of similar phrases with a partner and suggest more amusing alternatives.

Compare and contrast

12 Compare the humour displayed by Quentin Crisp with that of Bill Bryson (page 152). Do they have anything in common? How are they different?

Friendship

Lord Byron

GEORGE GORDON, Lord Byron (1788–1824), was one of the most famous poets of his day. His relationships with women were passionate, often disastrous and occasionally scandalous. He spent much of his life abroad but kept in touch with his friends and admirers via an astonishing volume of correspondence. He died at the Battle of Missolonghi, fighting for Greek independence.

To Lady Hardy

My dear "Cousin (*not*) of *Buckingham* and sage grave Woman"[1] it was my intention to have answered yr. letter sooner – but in the interim yr. Chevalier[2] arrived – and calling upon me had not been two minutes in the room (though I had not seen him for these nine years) before he began a long story about you – which I cut short as well as I could by telling him that I *knew* you – and was a *relative* and was not desirous of his confidence on the subject. He – however – persisted in declaring himself an illused Gentleman – and describing you – as a kind of cold Calypso[3] – who lead astray people of an amatory disposition[4] – without giving them any sort of

[1] ***Cousin of Buckingham, and sage, grave man:*** from *Richard III*, Act III, scene VII

[2] ***Chevalier:*** would-be lover

[3] ***Calypso:*** a sea nymph in Homer's *Odyssey* who detained Odysseus on her island for seven years

[4] ***amatory disposition:*** wanting to fall in love

compensation – contenting yourself it seems – with only making *one* fool – instead of *two* – which is the more approved method of proceeding on such occasions. – For my part – I think you quite right – and be assured from me that a woman who – (as Society is constituted in England –) gives any advantage to a man – may expect a lover – but will sooner or later find a tyrant. – And this may not perhaps be the Man's fault neither – but is the necessary and natural result of the Circumstances of Society which in fact tyrannize over the Man equally with the woman – that is to say if either of *them* have any feeling or honour. – He (the Chevalier) bored me so upon the subject that I greatly fear (Heaven forgive me for you won't) that I said something about the "transmutation[5] of hair" but I was surprised into it – by his wanting to [swear?] me out that his black wig – was the shock (or shocking) flaxen poodle furniture with which Nature had decorated his head ten years ago.

He is gone post to Leghorn[6] in pursuit of you – having (I presume in consequence of your disappearance) actually – (*no* jest I assure you) advertised "for an agreeable companion in a post-chaise" in the *Genoa Gazette*. – I enclose you the paragraph. – Have you found any benefit for your girl from the Leghorn Baths? or are you gone to Florence. – You can write to me at yr. own leisure and inclination. – I have always laid it down as a maxim – and found it justified by experience – that a man and a woman – make far better friendships than can exist between two of the same sex – but *then* with the condition – that they never

[5] ***transmutation:*** change
[6] ***Leghorn:*** the English name for the Italian town of Livorno

have made – or are to make love with each other. Lovers may be – and indeed generally are – enemies – but they never can be friends – because there must always be a spice of jealousy – and a something of Self in all their speculations. – Indeed I rather look upon Love altogether as a sort of hostile transaction – very necessary to make – or to break – matches and keep the world a-going-but by no means a sinecure[7] to the parties concerned. – Now – as *my* Love perils are – I believe pretty well over – and yours by all accounts are never to begin; – we shall be the best friends imaginable – as far as both are concerned – and with this advantage – that we may both fall to loving right and left through all our acquaintance – without either sullenness or sorrow from that amiable passion – which are it's [unnoble?] attributes. – I address this at hazard to Leghorn – believe me my dear Coz

ever & affectly yrs.
NB

[7] ***sinecure:*** a job which involves no work

Activities

Reading

1 What was Lady Hardy's crime according to her Chevalier?
2 How did Byron respond to his guest's stories about Lady Hardy?
3 Did he approve of his cousin's behaviour? Give reasons for your answer.
4 What, according to Byron, changes when men and women become lovers? Whose fault is this change?
5 What does Byron think about friendship between men and women?

Discussion

6 Do you agree with Byron's views on men and women? Is it possible for people of the opposite sex to be friends? Or does physical attraction always get in the way?
7 What impression of Byron's lifestyle do you form from this letter? Discuss your ideas in pairs or a small group.

Language study

8 Rewrite the first paragraph of this letter using more conventional punctuation, such as commas and full stops. When you have completed this task, compare your text with that of the letter. How does changing the punctuation affect your response?
9 Byron's letter is almost literally 'dashed off'. Discuss with a partner what you think of this style of punctuation. Do you find it confusing? Is it appropriate?

Writing

10 Write a paragraph using Byron's style of punctuation (you can write on any subject) using an appropriately 'gossipy' tone.

Death in Hebden Bridge

John Hillaby

TRAVEL writers go to extreme lengths to find exotic and interesting places to describe, but John Hillaby found a great deal worth observing in the small English town of Hebden Bridge.

FOUR locals, including a bus-conductor and a coalman, were discussing the obituaries in the *Hebden Bridge Times*, a staple topic[1] of conversation on Fridays.

Someone said Harry had gone out like a light. And wasn't that old neither he wasn't. Hardly seventy-four. Looked full o' fettle,[2] too. And he'd leave a packet, they reckoned.

"Bow-legged wi' brass[3] he was," one of them added.

"And won't be wanting me this winter," said the coalman, thoughtfully.

Nobody laughed, but if you looked hard you could see an almost imperceptible relaxation of jaw muscles which passes for amusement in the industrial Riding. Death had been cauterized[4] by a pungent platitude.[5] The macabre[6] humour stems from a long history of poverty when talk usually ranged round unemployment, the dole queue,

---

1 ***staple topic:*** a major subject for discussion
2 ***fettle:*** health
3 ***brass:*** money
4 ***cauterized:*** made less painful
5 ***platitude:*** an obvious remark
6 ***macabre:*** grim

sickness, and death. This survives still in an enormous repertoire of jokes calculated to horrify the stranger by the superficial denial of feeling.

"Where's t'wife?"

"Upstairs."

"Takin' it easy?"

"Aye. She's dead."

On this theme there are innumerable variations. One is of the neighbour who has come to pay his last respects. He stares long and earnestly at the deceased and says: "Well, I must say she looks pretty good." He pauses and then adds: "Considering." To this the husband says tartly, "And she ruddy well ought to. She's just had a week at Blackpool."[7]

Apocryphal these stories may be, but on the formalities of the laying-out, the interment, and the post mortem tea at the Co-operative café. I can speak with some authority, for I wrote about them as an apprentice on the nearby *Dewsbury District News*. We dealt in births, marriages, and deaths, especially deaths. This meant interviewing the relatives and following the mourners to the cemetery for the names on the wreaths. The paper abounded in names. Each one, the editor said, meant three readers. During one lean week in the funeral business, I recall writing a slightly facetious[8] biography of the cemetery-keeper, an elderly man who, I calculated, had put away about forty thousand of his fellow townsmen. The week after this piece of necrology[9] appeared in print I approached the man with some

[7] ***Blackpool:*** a popular holiday destination
[8] ***facetious:*** amusing but slightly inappropriate
[9] ***necrology:*** a list of people recently dead

circumspection, wondering if he had been offended by the article. Not a bit. He was delighted. "Ah've bin thinking about that there article o' thine," he said, "and ah'm gonna tell *thee* summat that might do thee a bit o' good."

He took me up to the highest point of the cemetery, where, with the air of a skilful gardener, he looked round carefully. Eventually he dug his heel into the ground and picked up a handful of earth, which he held under my nose. "Look, lad," he said. "That's *real* dry stuff. When your turn comes you get right down there. You'll last for *years*."

In addition to the obituary notices, we published little fragments of memorial verse which was not only paid for, but sometimes actually composed by the relatives. I recall one which ran:

Gabriel's trumpet sounded,
And God said, "Come!"
The Heavenly Gates opened
And in walked Mum.

Activities

Reading

1 What is shocking about the coalman's comment? Why did he make it?
2 Why do the people of Hebden Bridge tell jokes about death in general?
3 Why was the editor of the *Dewsbury District News* interested in deaths?
4 How did the cemetery-keeper respond to the article about his work? How did he reward John Hillaby?
5 Why do you think John Hillaby quotes the piece of verse from the gravestone? What attitude towards death and the afterlife does it show?

Discussion

6 Do you think that we take death too seriously today? Is it easier to make jokes about it if you believe in life after death? Or if it is a familiar experience? Share your ideas in small groups.

Language study

7 This extract quotes several examples of Yorkshire in the speech of the inhabitants of Hebden Bridge. Make a table like the one below:

Dialect word or phrase	Standard English equivalent	Code
T'	The	P
Brass		

When you have completed the first two columns, use the following codes in the third column:
P – expressions which simply show a difference in pronunciation
V – expressions which use a different vocabulary from standard English
G – expressions that use different grammar rules from those found in standard English.

8 Why do you think distinctive dialects are less common in this country than they used to be? Give as many reasons as you can.

Writing

9 Is there anything distinctive about your own speech community? For instance, are there words and expressions that only get used in your school or local area that you have to explain to newcomers? In some schools, even different year groups have particular ways of speaking. Write a brief description of some of the ways that your local speech differs from standard English. Or you could write a brief guide for newcomers to your area.

Queuing

Bill Bryson

BEHAVIOUR that seems normal and natural to the inhabitants of a country can strike outsiders completely differently. Here the American writer Bill Bryson describes the English habit of queuing with something like admiration.

SO let's talk about something heartening. Let's talk about John Fallows. One day in 1987 Fallows was standing at a window in a London bank waiting to be served when a would-be robber named Douglas Bath stepped in front of him, brandished a handgun and demanded money from the cashier. Outraged, Fallows told Bath to "bugger off" to the back of the line and wait his turn, to the presumed approving nods of others in the queue. Unprepared for this turn of events, Bath meekly departed from the bank empty-handed and was arrested a short distance away.

I bring this up here to make the point that if there is one golden quality that characterizes the British it is an innate sense of good manners and you defy it at your peril. Deference and a quiet consideration for others are such a fundamental part of British life, in fact, that few conversations could even start without them. Almost any encounter with a stranger begins with the words "I'm terribly sorry but" followed by a request of some sort – "could you tell me the way to Brighton," "help me find a shirt my size," "get your steamer trunk off my foot." And when you've fulfilled their request, they invariably offer a hesitant, apologetic smile and say sorry again, begging forgiveness for taking up your time or carelessly leaving their foot where your steamer trunk[1] clearly needed to go. I just love that.

As if to illustrate my point, when I checked out of the Caledonian[2] late the next morning, I arrived to find a woman ahead of me wearing a helpless look and saying to the receptionist: "I'm terribly sorry but I can't seem to get the television in my room to work." She had come all the way downstairs, you understand, to apologize to *them* for their TV not working. My heart swelled with feelings of warmth and fondness for this strange and unfathomable country.

And it is all done so instinctively, that's the other thing. I remember when I was still new to the country arriving at a railway station one day to find that just two of the dozen or so ticket windows were open. (For the benefit of foreign readers, I should explain that as a rule in Britain no matter how many windows there are in a bank, post office or rail station, only two of them will be open, except at very busy times, when just one will be open.) Both ticket windows were occupied. Now, in other countries one of two things would have happened. Either there would be a crush of customers at each window, all demanding simultaneous attention, or else there would be two slow-moving lines, each full of gloomy people convinced that the other line was moving faster.

Here in Britain, however, the waiting customers had

---

[1] ***steamer trunk:*** a large and heavy trunk

[2] ***the Caledonian:*** the hotel where the author was staying

spontaneously come up with a much more sensible and ingenious arrangement. They had formed a single line a few feet back from both windows. When either position became vacant, the customer at the head of the line would step up to it and the rest of the line would shuffle forward a space. It was a wonderfully fair and democratic approach and the remarkable thing was that no one had commanded it or even suggested it. It just happened.

Much the same sort of thing occurred now, for when the lady with the recalcitrant TV set had finished with her apology (which the receptionist, I must say, accepted with uncommonly good grace, going so far as to hint that if anything else in the woman's room was found to be out of order, she wasn't to blame herself for a minute), the receptionist turned to me and another gentleman who was also waiting and said, "Who's next?" and he and I went through an elaborate after-you, no-after-you, but-I-insist, well-that's-most-gracious-of-you routine, which made my heart swell further.

Activities

Reading

1 What does the story about John Fallows show about the British? Why does Bill Bryson find it heartening?

2 What effect is the author hoping to achieve by using the steamer trunk example?

3 Why is the word '*them*' in italics? What sort of response does Bill Bryson imply an American would have to the situation described?

4 In the discussion of the ticket window queue, what suggestion is there about why the British are so good at queuing?

5 What does the receptionist's response to the complaint reveal about her level of politeness? Why does Bill Bryson find the whole situation so absurd?

Discussion

6 Have you noticed that people queue differently when you have been abroad? Share your experiences with the rest of the class. Is Bill Bryson exaggerating about the British attitude to queuing, or have you had similar experiences?

7 Politeness can occasionally be absurd, but do you think it is important? Organize a class debate on the importance of good manners. Begin with speakers for and against the topic and then open the subject to a more general debate, with one person acting as chair.

Language study

8 This extract does not start at the beginning and move on to the end. Instead it is in several sections. The first section concerns an item of news and the second is a general comment on it. Describe the other sections of the extract. Quote the words Bill Bryson uses to let you know the time and place of each section.

9 Look at the endings to the four paragraphs in this extract. What do they have in common in terms of sentence length and content? Remind yourself of the opening sentence and comment on how these endings help to hold this non-chronological piece together.

Writing

10 Clearly Bill Bryson admires the way the British go about queuing. If you have travelled abroad, write about some aspect of life that you admire in the country you visited. Give examples of the kind of behaviour you have observed.

11 If you have not travelled outside your own country, describe an aspect of life at home that you think foreign people should appreciate, such as tea drinking or garden centres. Try to show what such institutions tell you about people's attitude to life.

Writers at Work

People who write for a living inevitably write about their writing; except in one case here in which the author writes about not writing. If you do the exercises at the back you will be able to write about writers writing about writing. This may seem a little extreme but thinking about writing is second only to writing itself as a way of improving your own work.

On Not Writing

Geoff Dyer

PEOPLE often say that they think that they have a book in them. In Geoff Dyer's case this turned out to be a book about not writing a book.

I had decided years earlier that I would one day write a book about D.H. Lawrence, a homage to the writer who had made me want to become a writer. It was a cherished ambition and as part of my preparation for realizing this cherished ambition I had avoided reading anything by Lawrence so that at some point in the future I could go back to him if not afresh then at least not rock-stale. I didn't want to go back to him passively, didn't want to pick up a copy of *Sons and Lovers* aimlessly, to pass the time. I wanted to read him with a purpose. Then, after years of avoiding Lawrence, I moved into the phase of what might be termed pre-preparation. I visited Eastwood, his birthplace, I read biographies, I amassed a hoard of photographs which I kept in a once-new document wallet, blue, on which I had written 'D.H.L.: Photos' in determined black ink. I even built up an impressive stack of notes with Lawrence vaguely in mind but these notes, it is obvious to me now, actually served not to prepare for and facilitate the writing of a book about Lawrence but to defer and postpone doing so. There is nothing unusual about this. All over the world people are taking notes as a way of postponing, putting off and standing in for. My case was more extreme for not only was taking notes about Lawrence a way of putting off writing a study of – and homage to – the writer who had made me want to become a writer, but this study I was putting off writing was itself a way of putting off and postponing another book.

Although I had made up my mind to write a book about Lawrence I had also made up my mind to write a novel, and while the decision to write the book about Lawrence was made later it had not entirely superseded that earlier decision. At first I'd had an overwhelming urge to write both books but these two desires had worn each other down to the point where I had no urge to write either. Writing them both at the same time was inconceivable and so these two equally overwhelming ambitions first wore each other down and then wiped each other out. As soon as I thought about working on the novel I fell to thinking that it would be much more enjoyable to write my study of Lawrence. As soon as I started making notes on Lawrence I realized I was probably sabotaging forever any chance of writing my novel which, more than any other book I had written, had to be written immediately, before another protracted bout of labour came between me and the idea for what I perceived as a rambling, sub-Bernhardian[1] rant of a novel. It was now or never. So I went from making notes on Lawrence to making notes for my novel, by which I mean I went from not working on my book about Lawrence to not working on the novel because all of this to-ing and fro-ing and note-taking actually meant that I never did any work on either book. All I did was switch between two – empty – files on

[1] ***sub-Bernhardian:*** like the works of Geoffrey Bernhard, a famously grumpy writer

my computer, one conveniently called C:\DHL, the other C:\NOVEL, and sent myself ping-ponging back and forth between them until, after an hour and a half of this, I would turn off the computer because the worst thing of all, I knew, was to wear myself out in this way. The best thing was to do nothing, to sit calmly, but there was no calm, of course: instead, I felt totally desolate because I realized that I was going to write neither my study of D.H. Lawrence nor my novel.

Eventually, when I could bear it no longer, I threw myself wholeheartedly into my study of Lawrence because, whereas my novel was going to take me further into myself, the Lawrence book – a sober academic study of Lawrence – would have the opposite effect of taking me out of myself.

Activities

Reading

1 What was special about D.H. Lawrence for Geoff Dyer?
2 Why did he no longer read any of D.H. Lawence's books
3 What did he do instead of research for his book about D.H. Lawrence?
4 What did his preparations really involve?
5 How did the D.H. Lawrence book interfere with Geoff Dyer's novel, and vice versa?
6 Do you think either book will ever get written based on the evidence in the passage?

Discussion

7 Do you agree with Geoff Dyer that making notes on something is simply a way of putting off working on the thing itself? Discuss your own note making in your group. Do you make notes all the time, before writing an essay for instance, or only when exams are approaching? What methods of note making do you use? Be prepared to report your ideas back to the rest of the class. You can make notes if you wish.
8 Do you put off work? What kind of things do you do to avoid it? Do computers make avoiding work easier? Share your work avoidance strategies with a partner or in a small group.

Language study

9 Look closely at the italicized words in the following sentences. How do the verbs change as the sentences progress? Which word signals the change? What mood do the adjectives indicate?

> I *visited* Eastwood, his birthplace, I *read* biographies, I *amassed* a hoard of photographs which I *kept* in a once-new document wallet, blue, on which I *had written* 'D.H.L.: Photos' in *determined* black ink. I even *built up* an *impressive* stack of notes with Lawrence *vaguely* in mind but these notes, it is obvious to me now, actually served *not to prepare for and facilitate* the writing of a book about Lawrence but *to defer and postpone* doing so.

Writing

10 Can you make not doing something as interesting as doing it? Write a short description of an occasion where you failed to get something done. Focus on the details of your frustrations and aim for a light-hearted tone.

Sherlock Holmes

Sir Arthur Conan Doyle

SHERLOCK HOLMES is perhaps the most famous fictional detective ever. Here, his creator, Sir Arthur Conan Doyle, talks about some of the difficulties that inventing such a successful character can cause.

PEOPLE have often asked me whether I knew the end of a Holmes story before I started it. Of course I do. One could not possibly steer a course if one did not know one's destination. The first thing is to get your idea. Having got that key idea one's next task is to conceal it and lay emphasis upon everything which can make for a different explanation. Holmes, however, can see all the fallacies of the alternatives, and arrives more or less dramatically at the true solution by steps which he can describe and justify. He shows his powers by what the South Americans now call "Sherlockholmitos", which means clever little deductions, which often have nothing to do with the matter in hand, but impress the reader with a general sense of power. The same effect is gained by his offhand allusion to other cases. Heaven knows how many titles I have thrown about in a casual way, and how many readers have begged me to satisfy their curiosity as to 'Rigoletto and his Abominable Wife', 'The Adventure of the Tired Captain', or 'The Curious Experience of the Patterson Family in the Island of Uffa'. Once or twice, as in 'The Adventure of the Second Stain', which in my judgment is one of the neatest of the stories, I did actually use the title years before I wrote a story to correspond.

There are some questions concerned with particular stories which turn up periodically from every quarter of the globe. In 'The Adventure of the Priory School' Holmes remarks in his offhand way that by looking at a bicycle track on a damp moor one can say which way it was heading. I had so many remonstrances upon this point, varying from pity to anger, that I took out my bicycle and tried. I had imagined that the observations of the way in which the track of the hind wheel overlaid the track of the front one when the machine was not running dead straight would show the direction. I found that my correspondents were right and I was wrong, for this would be the same whichever way the cycle was moving. On the other hand the real solution was much simpler, for on an undulating moor the wheels make a much deeper impression uphill and a more shallow one downhill, so Holmes was justified of his wisdom after all.

Sometimes I have got upon dangerous ground where I have taken risks through my own want of knowledge of the correct atmosphere. I have, for example, never been a racing man, and yet I ventured to write 'Silver Blaze', in which the mystery depends upon the laws of training and racing. The story is all right, and Holmes may have been at the top of his form, but my ignorance cries aloud to heaven. I read an excellent and very damaging criticism of the story in some sporting paper, written clearly by a man who *did* know, in which he explained the exact penalties which would have come upon every one concerned if they had acted as I described. Half would have been in jail and the other half warned off the turf for ever. However, I have never been nervous about details, and one must be masterful sometimes. When an alarmed Editor wrote to me once: "There is no second line of rails at that point," I answered, "I make one." On the other hand, there are cases where accuracy is essential.

I do not wish to be ungrateful to Holmes, who has been a good friend to me in many ways. If I have sometimes been inclined to weary of him it is because his character admits of no light or shade. He is a calculating machine, and anything you add to that simply weakens the effect. Thus the variety of the stories must depend upon the romance and compact handling of the plots. I would say a word for Watson also, who in the course of seven volumes never shows one gleam of humour or makes one single joke. To make a real character one must sacrifice everything to consistency and remember Goldsmith's criticism of Johnson that "he would make the little fishes talk like whales".

I do not think that I ever realized what a living actual personality Holmes had become to the more guileless readers, until I heard of the very pleasing story of the char-à-banc[1] of French schoolboys who, when asked what they wanted to see first in London, replied unanimously that they wanted to see Mr Holmes' lodgings in Baker Street. Many have asked me which house it is, but that is a point which for excellent reasons I will not decide.

There are certain Sherlock Holmes stories, apocryphal[2] I need not say, which go round and round the press and turn up at fixed intervals with the regularity of a comet.

[1] ***char-à-banc:*** a motor coach, usually one used for sightseeing tours
[2] ***apocryphal:*** of questionable authenticity or untrue

One is the story of the cabman who is supposed to have taken me to an hotel in Paris. "Dr Doyle," he cried, gazing at me fixedly, "I perceive from your appearance that you have been recently at Constantinople. I have reason to think also that you have been at Buda, and I perceive some indication that you were not far from Milan." "Wonderful. Five francs for the secret of how you did it?" "I looked at the labels pasted on your trunk," said the astute cabby.

Another perennial is of the woman who is said to have consulted Sherlock. "I am greatly puzzled, sir. In one week I have lost a motor horn, a brush, a box of golf balls, a dictionary and a bootjack. Can you explain it?" "Nothing simpler, madame," said Sherlock. "It is clear that your neighbour keeps a goat."

There was a third about how Sherlock entered heaven, and by virtue of his power of observation at once greeted Adam, but the point is perhaps too anatomical for further discussion.

Activities

Reading

1 Briefly describe Sir Arthur Conan Doyle's method of composing a Sherlock Holmes story.
2 How is Sherlock Holmes made to look powerful?
3 What kinds of comments got Conan Doyle into trouble with his readers?
4 What was his attitude to inventing details?
5 What did Sir Arthur Conan Doyle dislike about Sherlock Holmes? Why didn't he change him?
6 What do the stories Conan Doyle has heard indicate about many people's response to fiction?

Discussion

7 Have you ever read a Sherlock Holmes story, or seen a film or television version? Why do you think the character of Sherlock Holmes has been so successful? In groups, talk about the stories you know and discuss what makes them entertaining.
8 Sir Arthur Conan Doyle states that he has 'sometimes been inclined to weary' of Sherlock Holmes. Do you think this is a common problem for successful artistic creations? Do bands get tired of playing their greatest hit? Is J.K. Rowling tired of Harry Potter? What tension between writer and audience does success create?

Language study

9 Sir Arthur Conan Doyle mentions the titles of several Sherlock Holmes adventures in this account, most of which he didn't actually write but which his readers wanted to read. Find and discuss the titles with a partner and decide on what techniques Conan Doyle used to arouse his readers' curiosity. If you know the titles of any other Sherlock Holmes stories, you can add them to the list.
10 Having explored Conan Doyle's title writing techniques, compose one or two yourself and then share them with the class. Which title sounds most like a Sherlock Holmes story? Why?

Writing

11 Using your answer to question 1, write a detective story which follows Sir Arthur Conan Doyle's advice. You can feature Sherlock Holmes and Dr Watson if you wish, or you could choose a more modern setting.

Experience

Martin Amis

LITERARY ability does not seem to be inherited as often as, say, musical talent and there are very few examples of parents and children being successful novelists. The exception to this rule is provided by Kingsley and Martin Amis.

WE sat in high-bourgeois[1] splendour, my father and I, in the house outside Barnet, having a pre-lunch drink and talking about his first published story, *The Sacred Rhino of Uganda* (1932: he was ten). Now it was 1972, and he had just turned fifty, an occasion he marked with a poem: 'Ode to Me' ('Fifty today, old lad?/Well, that's not doing so bad ...'). He was then at the height of his prosperity and productiveness; and his marriage to Jane was still cloudless – or so, at any rate, I believed. *The Sacred Rhino of Uganda*:

– It was awful in all the usual ways. And full of false quantities.[2] Things like: 'Raging and cursing in the blazing heat ...'

– What's wrong with that? I mean I can see it's old fashioned ...

– You can't have three *ings* like that.

– Can't you?

– No. It would have to be: 'Raging and cursing in the ... intolerable heat.'

[1] ***high-bourgeois:*** middle class
[2] ***quantities:*** sounds of similar duration

You couldn't have three *ings* like that. And sometimes you couldn't even have two. The same went for *-ics, -ives, -lys* and *-tions*. And the same went for all prefixes too.

After lunch I went up to my room and spent a few hours with the novel I was about to submit for publication. Later, over a pre-dinner drink, I said,

– I've been going through my book. And guess what. It's doggerel.[3]

– I'm sure it's not.

– It is. It's all 'the cook took a look at the book'. It's like a nursery rhyme. Hickory dickory dock, the mouse ran up the clock.

– You're exaggerating.

Yes, but I did revise the novel yet again: making war on the *-ings* and the *-ics*, the *pre*s and the *pro*s.

It was the only piece of literary counsel he ever gave me. And, of course, he had never expressed any desire that I should pursue the literary life, despite all the evidence that I had such a life in mind. I attributed this to sheer indolence[4] on his part, but I now think he was obeying a parental instinct, and a good one. Five years later, when I was back-half editor of the *New Statesman*, a well-known writer visited me in my office with his son. The boy (seventeen?) wrote poems, it was explained, and the father wanted me to look at them; perhaps I might accept one or two for publication. I was ten years older than the poet. I sympathized with him. But I think I pointed out immediately that nobody writing in English had ever done anything of much merit before the age of about twenty (no,

---

[3] ***doggerel***: poor-quality verse
[4] ***indolence:*** laziness

not even poor Thomas Chatterton,[5] 'the marvellous boy', who was seventeen – and destitute, after early successes – when he poisoned himself with arsenic). The well-known writer gently persisted. And I thought, all right, it's conceivable: Rimbaud[6] was the same age when he wrote *Le Bateau Ivre*. I looked at the son's poems. And I sent them back to him with a letter saying that I thought they were promising, and (equally truthfully) that I would be happy to keep an eye on his stuff as it came along ...

In the arts, when the parent invites the child to follow – this is a complicated offer, and there will always be a suspicion of egotism in it. Is the child's promise a tribute to the superabundance of the father's gift? And historically what long odds you face; there's Mrs Trollope as well as Anthony, and Dumas *pere et fils*, and that's about it. What usually happens is that the child is productive for a while, and then the filial rivalrousness plays itself out. I think literary talent is strongly inherited. But literary stamina is not.

---

[5] ***Thomas Chatterton:*** 1752–70, British poet who wrote mock medieval verse and prose. He committed suicide at the age of 17.

[6] ***Rimbaud:*** Arthur Rimbaud 1854–91, French poet. He abandoned writing aged about 20 and spent the rest of his life travelling.

Activities

Reading

1 What was wrong with Kingsley Amis's first published story?
2 Do you agree with Kingsley Amis's judgement on '-ings' and other endings?
3 What was Martin Amis's response to his father's comments?
4 Give reasons for Kingsley Amis not encouraging his son's career as a novelist.
5 What did historical example seem to show about Martin Amis' chance of success?
6 Martin Amis seems to imply that some novelists' children do get published, but why are they not as successful as their parents?

Discussion

7 Do you think following your parents' choice of career is a good idea? What are the advantages and disadvantages? Share your thoughts in your group.
8 What 'literary counsel' would you give to other writers? In small groups, compile as many pieces of good advice about writing as you can and then write up the two or three best pieces of advice for a wall display.

Language study

9 Do you think Martin Amis is being slightly mischievous in quoting his father's poem? What fault might it be accused of?
10 Try out Kingsley Amis's advice. Write a sentence or two using a several '-ings', '-ics', '-ves', '-lys' or '-tions' in a row. Do your sentences sound unnatural? If you think they do, how might you rewrite them?

Writing

11 Kingsley Amis seems to have been successful, on this one occasion, in giving advice to his son. Many parents are not so fortunate. Write a magazine article aimed at parents on: How to Give Advice to Your Children. You should think beforehand of occasions when you have followed your parents' advice and times when you have found it annoying. You can then apply some general rules on what kind of advice succeeds and how it is best delivered.

Compare and contrast

12 Sir Arthur Conan Doyle is tired of Sherlock Holmes, Geoff Dyer can't get started on his books and both Amis's speak poorly of their work. Discuss whether you think being a writer is a good choice of profession. Use evidence from the writers in this section and give as many reasons for and against as you can.

Activities Mapping

English Framework Objectives (Year 7/8/9)

Extract Title and Main Text Type	Word (W) & Sentence (S) Level	Reading Text Level	Writing Text Level	Speaking & Listening
Illness and Disability				
Meeting Francesca Recount (Autobiography) Post-1914	**(7)** S12, S13, S14, S15, S17 **(8)** W12, W13; S7, S8, S12 **(9)** W7; S3, S4, S7, S9	**(7)** 1, 4, 6, 7, 8, 14 **(8)** 7, 10 **(9)** 6, 7, 11	**(7)** 1, 2, 10, 11, 12, 15, 19 **(8)** 2, 10, 14, 17 **(9)** 10, 16, 17	**(7)** 5, 12, 13, 14 **(8)** 5, 10
My Brother Recount Post-1914	**(7)** S8, S12, S13, S14, S15, S17 **(8)** W12, W13; S2, S6, S7, S8, S12 **(9)** W7; S3, S4, S7, S9	**(7)** 1, 4, 6, 7, 8, 14 **(8)** 7, 10 **(9)** 6, 7, 11	**(7)** 1, 2, 6, 8, 14, 15, 19 **(8)** 2, 6, 10, 14, 17 **(9)** 10, 11, 16, 17	**(7)** 5, 12, 13, 14 **(8)** 5, 10
Locked In Recount (Autobiography) Post-1914	**(7)** W14, W17; S8, S9, S12 **(8)** W8, W11; S2, S7 **(9)** W6, W7	**(7)** 1, 4, 6, 7, 8, 14, 15 **(8)** 7, 10 **(9)** 6, 11	**(7)** 1, 2, 8, 11 **(8)** 2, 6, 7, 10 **(9)** 6, 11, 12	**(7)** 5, 12, 13, 14 **(8)** 5, 10
Contact Recount (Autobiography) Post-1914	**(7)** W14; S7, S11, S12 **(8)** S2, S7 **(9)** W7; S4	**(7)** 1, 4, 6, 7, 8, 14, 15 **(8)** 7, 10 **(9)** 6, 7, 11	**(7)** 1, 2, 3, 5, 6, 7, 8, 10, 11, 12, 16, 19 **(8)** 2, 5, 6, 7, 10, 17 **(9)** 5, 9, 17	**(7)** 5, 11, 12, 13, 14 **(8)** 10, 11, 12 **(9)** 9

Extract Title and Main Text Type	Word (W) & Sentence (S) Level	Reading Text Level	Writing Text Level	Speaking & Listening
Encounters with Animal				
On Yeti Tracks Recount (Travel) Post-1914	**(7)** W14; S3, S5, S11, S12, S14, S15, S17 **(8)** W12; S1, S3, S9, S12 **(9)** W7; S2, S3, S5	**(7)** 1, 4, 6, 7, 8, 12, 13, 14, 15 **(8)** 5, 6, 7, 10 **(9)** 6, 7	**(7)** 1, 2, 3, 10, 11, 12, 14 **(8)** 2, 10, 13, 17 **(9)** 4, 7, 9, 11, 12	**(7)** 5, 11, 12, 13, 14 **(8)** 5, 10, 11, 12 **(9)** 9
Spiders and Snakes Recount (Autobiography) Post-1914	**(7)** W14; S3, S5, S11, S12, S14, S15, S17 **(8)** W11, W12; S1, S3, S9, S12 **(9)** W7; S2, S3, S5	**(7)** 1, 4, 6, 7, 8, 9, 12, 13, 14, 15 **(8)** 5, 6, 7, 10, 11 **(9)** 4, 5, 6, 7	**(7)** 1, 2, 3, 6, 7, 8, 10, 11, 12, 14 **(8)** 1, 2, 5, 6, 7, 10, 12 **(9)** 4, 5, 6, 7, 9, 11	**(7)** 5, 11, 12, 13 **(8)** 5, 10, 12
Scorpion Recount (Autobiography) Post-1914	**(7)** W14, W22; S3, S5, S11, S12, S14, S15, S17 **(8)** W11, W12; S1, S3, S9, S12, S14 **(9)** W7; S2, S3, S5	**(7)** 1, 4, 6, 7, 8, 9, 12, 13, 14, 15 **(8)** 5, 6, 7, 10, 11 **(9)** 4, 5, 6, 7	**(7)** 1, 2, 3, 6, 7, 8 **(8)** 1, 2, 5, 6, 7 **(9)** 4, 5, 6, 7, 12	**(7)** 5, 11, 12, 13 **(8)** 5, 10, 12

Extract Title and Main Text Type	Word (W) & Sentence (S) Level	Reading Text Level	Writing Text Level	Speaking & Listening
War				
Arrests Recount (Diary) Post-1914	**(7)** W14; S12, S14, S15, S17 **(8)** W11, W12, W13; S8, S12 **(9)** W7; S3, S4	**(7)** 1, 4, 6, 7, 8, 9, 13 , 14, 15 **(8)** 5, 6, 7, 10, 11 **(9)** 6, 7, 9, 11	**(7)** 1, 2, 3, 11, 12, 15, 16, 17 **(8)** 1, 2, 10, 13, 14, 15 **(9)** 1, 4, 12, 13, 15	**(7)** 5, 11, 12, 13 **(8)** 5, 10, 12
The End Recount (Autobiography) Post-1914	**(7)** S1, S11 **(8)** W11; S1, S2 **(9)** W7	**(7)** 1, 4, 6, 7, 8, 9, 13, 14, 15 **(8)** 5, 6, 7, 10, 11 **(9)** 6, 7, 9, 11	**(7)** 3, 10, 12, 14, 19 **(8)** 1, 2, 5, 7, 12, 17 **(9)** 5, 7, 11, 16, 17	**(7)** 5, 11, 12, 13 **(8)** 5, 10, 12
In the Trenches Recount (Autobiography) Pre-1914	**(7)** S5, S8, S9, S10, S11, S12, S14, S15 **(8)** W12, W13; S1, S2, S6, S7, S8, S12 **(9)** W7; S3, S4, S6	**(7)** 1, 4, 6, 7, 8, 9, 13, 14, 15 **(8)** 5, 6, 7, 10, 11 **(9)** 6, 7, 9, 11	**(7)** 1, 2, 3, 6, 7, 8, 9, 10, 11, 14 **(8)** 1, 2, 5, 6, 7, 12 **(9)** 5, 7, 11	**(7)** 5, 12, 13, 14 **(8)** 10, 11

Extract Title and Main Text Type	Word (W) & Sentence (S) Level	Reading Text Level	Writing Text Level	Speaking & Listening
Death				
Before I Say Goodbye Recount (Diary) Post-1914	**(7)** S11, S12, S13, S15 **(8)** W7, W11, W12, W13; S7, S8 **(9)** W7; S3, S4	**(7)** 1, 4, 6, 7, 8, 13, 14 **(8)** 5, 6, 7, 10, 11 **(9)** 6, 7, 11	**(7)** 1, 2, 6, 7, 8, 11 **(8)** 2, 5, 6, 7, 10 **(9)** 5, 6, 7, 11, 12	**(7)** 5, 12, 13, 14 **(8)** 10, 11
Death in the Family Recount (Autobiography) Pre-1914	**(7)** S11, S12, S13 **(8)** S6, S7 **(9)** W7; S3, S4, S6	**(7)** 1, 4, 6, 7, 8, 13, 14 **(8)** 5, 6, 7, 10, 11 **(9)** 6, 7, 9, 11	**(7)** 1, 2, 6, 7, 8, 10, 11, 19 **(8)** 2, 5, 6, 7, 10, 17 **(9)** 5, 6, 7, 9, 11, 12, 16, 17	**(7)** 5, 7, 11, 12, 13, 14 **(8)** 2, 10, 11, 12 **(9)** 2, 8, 9, 10
In Prison Recount (Autobiography) Post-1914	**(7)** S11, S12, S13, S15 **(8)** W7, W11, W12, W13; S2, S7, S8 **(9)** W7; S3, S4	**(7)** 1, 4, 6, 7, 8, 13, 14 **(8)** 5, 6, 7, 10, 11 **(9)** 6, 7, 9, 11	**(7)** 1, 2, 6, 7, 8, 11 **(8)** 2, 5, 6, 7, 10 **(9)** 5, 6, 7, 11, 12	**(7)** 5, 11, 12, 13, 14 **(8)** 5, 7, 10, 11, 12 **(9)** 9

Extract Title and Main Text Type	Word (W) & Sentence (S) Level	Reading Text Level	Writing Text Level	Speaking & Listening
Birth, Childhood and Parents				
Forty Weeks Recount (Autobiography) Post-1914	**(7)** S12, S13, S17 **(8)** W11, W12, W13; S6, S8	**(7)** 1, 4, 6, 7, 8, 13, 14 **(8)** 5, 6, 7, 10, 11 **(9)** 6, 7, 9, 11	**(7)** 2, 3, 6, 9, 10, 11, 12, 14 **(8)** 2, 10, 12, 17 **(9)** 9, 11, 12	**(7)** 5, 7, 11, 12, 13, 14 **(8)** 2, 10, 11, 12 **(9)** 2, 8, 9, 10
Childbirth Recount (Autobiography) Post-1914	**(7)** S8, S12, S13, S15, S17 **(8)** W11, W12, W13; S6, S8, S12 **(9)** W7; S3, S4, S9	**(7)** 1, 4, 6, 7, 8, 13, 14 **(8)** 5, 6, 7, 10, 11 **(9)** 6, 7, 9, 11	**(7)** 2, 11, 19 **(8)** 2, 10, 17 **(9)** 16, 17	**(7)** 5, 7, 11, 12, 13, 14 **(8)** 2, 10, 11, 12 **(9)** 2, 8, 9, 10
Disappearing Mother Recount (Autobiography) Post-1914	**(7)** W7; S11, S12, S13, S15 **(8)** W7, W8, W11, W12, W13; S7, S8 **(9)** W7; S3, S4	**(7)** 1, 4, 6, 7, 8, 13, 14 **(8)** 5, 6, 7, 10, 11 **(9)** 6, 7, 9, 11	**(7)** 1, 2, 6, 7, 8, 11 **(8)** 2, 5, 6, 7, 10 **(9)** 5, 6, 7, 11, 12	**(7)** 5, 11, 12, 13, 14 **(8)** 10, 11, 12 **(9)** 9
Father and Son Recount (Autobiography) Pre-1914	**(7)** S11, S12, S13, S15 **(8)** W7, W11, W12, W13; S7, S8 **(9)** W7; S3, S4	**(7)** 1, 2, 4, 6, 7, 8, 13, 14 **(8)** 2, 3, 5, 6, 7, 10, 11 **(9)** 6, 7, 9	**(7)** 1, 2, 6, 9, 11, 12, 19 **(8)** 2, 5, 6, 7, 10, 16, 17 **(9)** 4, 9, 11, 12, 16, 17	**(7)** 5, 12, 13, 14 **(8)** 10, 11

Extract Title and Main Text Type	Word (W) & Sentence (S) Level	Reading Text Level	Writing Text Level	Speaking & Listening
School				
A Welsh Childhood Recount (Autobiography) Post-1914	**(7)** W14; S8, S12 **(8)** W14; S1, S2, S3, S7 **(9)** W7; S4, S11	**(7)** 1, 2, 4, 6, 7, 8, 13, 14 **(8)** 2, 3, 5, 6, 7, 10, 11 **(9)** 6, 7, 9	**(7)** 1, 2, 6, 8, 14 **(8)** 2, 6, 7, **(9)** 6, 11	**(7)** 5, 12, 13, 14 **(8)** 10, 11
An Italian Education Recount Post-1914	**(7)** W14; S8, S11, S12, S13, S15 **(8)** W11, W12, W13; S2, S6, S7, S8 **(9)** W7; S3, S4, S9	**(7)** 1, 2, 4, 6, 7, 8, 9, 12, 13, 14 **(8)** 5, 6, 7, 10, 11 **(9)** 6, 7, 9	**(7)** 1, 2, 3, 10, 11, 12, 14, 16, 18, 19 **(8)** 1, 2, 10, 12, 16, 17 **(9)** 2, 4, 7, 9, 10, 11, 12, 16, 17	**(7)** 5, 11, 12, 13, 14 **(8)** 10, 11
At School in Ireland Recount Post-1914	**(7)** W14, W17, W20; S8, S11, S12, S14, S17 **(8)** S1, S7, S8 **(9)** W7; S3, S7, S9	**(7)** 1, 2, 4, 6, 7, 8, 9, 13, 14 **(8)** 5, 6, 7, 10, 11 **(9)** 6, 7, 9	**(7)** 1, 2, 3, 5, 6, 7, 8, 14 **(8)** 1, 2, 5, 6, 7 **(9)** 5, 6, 7	**(7)** 2 **(8)** 2, 7

Extract Title and Main Text Type	Word (W) & Sentence (S) Level	Reading Text Level	Writing Text Level	Speaking & Listening
Places				
Daffodils and *I Wandered Lonely as a Cloud* Recount (Diary) & Poem Pre-1914	**(7)** W14; S8, S12 **(8)** W11, W12; S2, S12 **(9)** W7; S3, S11	**(7)** 1, 2, 4, 6, 7, 8, 9, 13, 14 **(8)** 5, 6, 7, 10, 11 **(9)** 6, 7	**(7)** 1, 2, 6, 10, 11, 14 **(8)** 2, 10, 17 **(9)** 9, 11, 16, 17	**(7)** 5, 12, 13, 14 **(8)** 5, 10, 11 **(9)** 2, 5, 9
Lark Rise Recount (Autobiography) Post-1914	**(7)** W14; S8, S12 **(8)** W11, W12; S2, S12 **(9)** W7; S3, S11	**(7)** 1, 2, 4, 6, 7, 8, 9, 13, 14 **(8)** 5, 6, 7, 10, 11 **(9)** 6, 7, 9	**(7)** 1, 2, 6, 7, 8, 10, 11, 14, 19 **(8)** 2, 6, 7, 10, 17 **(9)** 2, 6, 9, 16, 17	**(7)** 5, 12, 13, 14 **(8)** 5, 10, 11
Iron Country Recount (Journal – Travel) Pre-1914	**(7)** W14; S8, S12 **(8)** W11, W12; S2, S12 **(9)** W7; S3, S11	**(7)** 1, 2, 4, 6, 7, 8, 9, 13, 14 **(8)** 5, 6, 7, 10, 11 **(9)** 6, 7	**(7)** 1, 2, 11, 12, 14 **(8)** 2, 5, 6, 7 **(9)** 6, 11, 12, 17	**(7)** 5, 11, 12, 13, 14 **(8)** 5, 10, 11, 12

Extract Title and Main Text Type	Word (W) & Sentence (S) Level	Reading Text Level	Writing Text Level	Speaking & Listening
People				
Being a Model Recount (Autobiography) Post-1914	**(7)** W14; S8, S12 **(8)** W11, W12; S2, S12 **(9)** W7; S3, S11	**(7)** 1, 2, 4, 6, 7, 8, 9, 13, 14 **(8)** 5, 6, 7, 10, 11 **(9)** 6, 7	**(7)** 1, 2, 10, 11, 19 **(8)** 2, 3, 10, 17 **(9)** 9, 16, 17	**(7)** 5, 11, 12, 13, 14 **(8)** 5, 10, 11, 12
Friendship Recount (Letter) Pre-1914	**(7)** S1, S3, S15 **(8)** S1, S2, S3 **(9)** W7; S1, S2, S3, S4	**(7)** 1, 2, 4, 6, 7, 8, 9, 13, 14 **(8)** 5, 6, 7, 10, 11 **(9)** 6, 7	**(7)** 3	**(7)** 5, 11, 12, 13, 14 **(8)** 5, 10, 11
Death in Hebden Bridge Recount Post-1914	**(7)** W14, W16; S8 S12, S13, S14, S15, S16 **(8)** W7, W9, W12; S9, S11, S12 **(9)** W7; S4, S10	**(7)** 1, 2, 4, 6, 7, 8, 9, 13, 14 **(8)** 5, 6, 7, 10, 11 **(9)** 6, 7	**(7)** 1, 2, 10, 11 **(8)** 2, 10, 12, 17 **(9)** 4, 9	**(7)** 5, 11,12, 13, 14 **(8)** 5, 10, 11, 12
Queuing Recount (Travel) Post-1914	**(7)** W14; S8, S9, S10, S11, S12, S15 **(8)** W11, W12; S6 **(9)** W7; S3, S6, S9	**(7)** 1, 2, 4, 6, 7, 8, 9, 13, 14 **(8)** 5, 6, 7, 10, 11 **(9)** 6, 7	**(7)** 1, 2, 3, 6, 7, 8, 9, 10, 11, 14 **(8)** 1, 2, 5, 6, 7, 12 **(9)** 5, 7, 11	**(7)** 3, 4, 5, 6, 7, 11, 12, 13, 14 **(8)** 3, 5, 6, 7, 10, 11, 12 **(9)** 2, 5, 6, 7, 9

Extract Title and Main Text Type	Word (W) & Sentence (S) Level	Reading Text Level	Writing Text Level	Speaking & Listening
at Work				
On Not Writing Recount (Autobiography) Post-1914	**(7)** W14, W17; S8, S12, S15 **(8)** W8, W12, W13; S2, S4, S9, S12 **(9)** W7; S3, S9	**(7)** 1, 2, 4, 6, 7, 8, 9, 13, 14 **(8)** 5, 6, 7, 10, 11 **(9)** 6, 7, 11, 12	**(7)** 1, 2, 6, 11 **(8)** 1, 2, 7, 12 **(9)** 6, 7, 11	**(7)** 5, 12, 13, 14 **(8)** 5, 10, 11
Sherlock Holmes Recount (Autobiography) Pre-1914	**(7)** W14; S7, S8, S11, S12, S17 **(8)** W13; S2, S3, S7 **(9)** W7; S2, S3, S4, S9	**(7)** 1, 2, 4, 6, 7, 8, 9, 13 **(8)** 5, 6, 7, 10 **(9)** 11	**(7)** 1, 2, 5, 6, 7, 8, 9, 10 **(8)** 1, 2, 5, 6, 7, 8, 17 **(9)** 5	**(7)** 5, 11,12, 13, 14 **(8)** 5, 10, 11
Experience Recount (Autobiography) Post-1914	**(7)** W14; S7, S8, S11, S12, S17 **(8)** W13; S2, S3, S7 **(9)** W7; S2, S3, S4, S9	**(7)** 1, 2, 4, 6, 7, 8, 9, 13 **(8)** 5, 6, 7, 10, 11 **(9)** 6, 7, 11	**(7)** 1, 2, 10, 11, 12, 15, 16, 17, 18, 19 **(8)** 2, 10, 13, 14, 17 **(9)** 4, 12, 13, 15, 16, 17	**(7)** 5, 11,12, 13, 14 **(8)** 5, 10, 11

Acknowledgements

The author and publishers wish to thank the following for permission to use copyright material:

Carcanet Press for material from Robert Graves, *Goodbye to All That* (1929) pp. 176–8

Curtis Brown on behalf of the Estate of the author for material from Gerald Durrell, *My Family and Other Animals* (1956) pp. 53–4;

Gillon Aitken Associates Ltd on behalf of the Estate of the author for material from Bruce Chatwin, *What Am I Doing Here?*, Jonathan Cape (1989) pp. 279–83. Copyright © Bruce Chatwin 1988

Granta Books for material from Jenny Diski, *Skating to Antarctica* (1997) pp. 24–7

John Murray (Publishers) Ltd for material from *Byron's Letters and Journals, Vol. 10* (1980) pp. 49–50

HarperCollins Publishers for material from Jean Dominique Bauby, *The Diving-Bell and the Butterfly* (1997) pp. 11–14; Lorna Sage, *Bad Blood*, Fourth Estate (2000) pp. 258–61; and Quentin Crisp, *The Naked Civil Servant*, Flamingo (1968) pp. 132–5

The Orion Publishing Group Ltd for material from Edna O'Brien, *Mother Ireland*, Penguin (1978) pp. 41–5

Oxford University Press for material from *Journals of Dorothy Wordsworth: The Alfoxden Journal, 1798, The Grasmere Journals, 1800–1803*, ed. Mary Moorman, 2nd edition (1971); and Flora Thompson, *Lark Rise to Candleford* (1945) pp. 18–21

PFD on behalf of the author for material from Clive James, *Unreliable Memoirs*, Pan Books (1980) pp. 20–22

The Penguin Group for material from Ruth Picardie, with Matt Seaton and Justine Picardie, *Before I Say Goodbye*, (1998) pp. 76–9. Copyright © Ruth Picardie 1997; Maxim Gorky, *My Childhood*, trs. Ronald Wilks, Penguin Classics (1966) pp. 15–18. Translation copyright © Ronald Wilks, 1966; Alice Thomas Ellis, *A Welsh Childhood*, (1990) pp. 12–3. Copyright © Alice Thomas Ellis 1990; and Anne Frank, *The Diary of a Young Girl: The Definitive Edition*, eds. Otto H. Frank and Miriam Pressier, trs. Susan Massotty, Viking (1997). Copyright © The Anne Frank-Fonds, Basle, Switzerland 1991. English copyright © Doubleday, a division of Bantam Doubleday Dell Publishing Group Inc, 1995

The Random House Group Ltd for material from Christy Brown, *My Left Foot*, Secker & Warburg (1954) pp. 16–7; Primo Levi, *The Truce*, Bodley Head, pp. 190–3; Martin Amos, *Experience*, Jonathan Cape (2000) pp. 22. 23; and Tim Parks, *An Italian Education*, Secker & Warburg (1996) pp. 286–91

Shawn Slovo for material from Ruth First, *One Hundred and Seventeen Days*, Penguin (1965) pp. 130–2

Time Warner Books UK for material from Geoff Dyer, *Out of Sheer Rage*, Little Brown (1997 pp. 2–3

Transworld Publishers, a division of the Random House Group Ltd, for material from Bill Bryson, *Notes From a Small Island*, Black Swan (1996) pp. 311–3. Copyright © Bill Bryson 1995; and Elizabeth Luard, *Family Life* (1996) pp. 262–5. Copyright © Elizabeth Luard 1996

A. P. Watt Ltd on behalf of The National Trust for Places of Historical Interest or Natural Beauty for material from Rachel Cusk, *A Life's Work*, Fourth Estate, pp. 38–40

The Wylie Agency (UK) Ltd on behalf of the author for material from Jamaica Kincaid, *My Brother*, Noonday Press (1997) pp. 92–6

Every effort has been made to trace the copyright holders but if any have been inadvertently overlooked the publishers will be pleased to make the necessary arrangement at the first opportunity.

Collins Cascades

Other titles in the **Collins** *Cascades series that you might enjoy:*

Miles Ahead: A Cascades collection of travel writing

ED. WENDY COOLING

This selection of the most entertaining and inspiring travel writing has been edited by Wendy Cooling, widely known in schools for her work as a literary consultant.

ISBN 000 711 259 9

As it Happens: A Cascades collection of reportage

ED. ROSY BORDER

Fascinating and occasionally unbelievable first-hand accounts of great events, terrible situations and epic discoveries, selected by an experienced author and former journalist.

ISBN 000 711 364 1

War Stories: A Cascades collection of fiction and non-fiction

ED. CHRISTOPHER MARTIN

This collection, from the author of the bestselling *War Poems*, features accounts of war and its impact on human lives from before and after 1914, written by men and women.

ISBN 000 711 485 0